Catching Success

Fishing, Leadership, and Relationships

Dewey E. Johnson

Catching Success: Fishing, Leadership, and Relationships

Copyright @ 2001 by Dewey E. Johnson
Printed by Jostens, Visalia, California.
This book may not be reproduced or transmitted in whole or in part, in any form or by any means, electronic or mechanical, including photocopying, recording or by any information storage and retrieval system, without the prior written permission of the author except for the inclusion of brief quotations in a review. All rights reserved.

Library of Congress Cataloging-in-Publication Data

Johnson, Dewey E.
Catching Success: Fishing, Leadership, and Relationships
Dewey E. Johnson/ 1st Ed.
   p. cm.
      Includes illustrations, glossary
      LCCN: 00-192425; SAN: 253-5157;
      ISBN 0-9705192-6-5

   1. Fishing.   2. Leadership.   3. Relationships.

   SH463.J63   799.1

Catching Success Press
6541 N. Ricewood, Fresno, CA 93711
www.catchingsuccess.com

PRINTED IN THE UNITED STATES OF AMERICA

Catching Success

Fishing, Leadership, and Relationships

Dewey E. Johnson

Table of Contents

Introduction & Acknowledgements .... *vii*

Catching Success

Catching Success 1
Searching For The Big One 5
Fish Where The Fish Are Running 9
The Channel 13
The Best Don't Always Finish First 17

Catching Success Through Leadership

Matching The Hatch 21
Clean The Weeds 25
Tying A Loop 29
Too Much Plastic 33
The "Muskie 8" Technique 37
Your Tackle Box Is A Paper Bag 41
The Practice Pool 45
Fish Can't Tell The Gender 49
Learning From The Kids 53
Let The Guide, Guide 57
Sort Your Tackle Box 61
Riding In The Passenger Seat 65
More Than A Pretty Face 69
Great Pitch 73
Thunder Drives Them Deep 77
Triggering A Response 81
The Favorite Fishing Spot 85
The Lesson 89
The Walking Egret 93

Catching Success Through Change

Making A Change 97
Reading The Turbulent Waters 101
The Past May Not Be The Future 105
The Weather Channel 109
Trolling The Windy Shore 113

Catching Success Through Relationships

Fishing Is For Relationships 119
Shore Lunch Values 123
Watching Them Bite 127
You Get What You Give 131
Let The Eagles Fly 135
Every Island Has Opportunities 139
Happy To Catch Just One 143
Sensitizing Your Bobber 147
Better Bring A Sandwich 151
A Day Meant To Be Shared 155
When Trouble Strikes 159
Targeting The Generations 163
Overcoming Disappointment 167

Reflections on Catching Success

How Many Did You Catch? 173
All Others Are Bait 177
Being The One 181
Afterthoughts 185

Glossary *187*
About The Author *195*
Order Forms *197*

Introduction and Acknowledgements

There are thousands of books on leadership and thousands of books on fishing. This book is unique because it looks at leadership from a fishing perspective and fishing from a leadership perspective. It is also a book about relationships–providing insights on how to develop more effective interactions with others and the world around you.

The leadership wisdom is based on the practical experience of leaders, past and present. The fishing wisdom is also based on the practical experience of many skilled anglers. I believe it is important to preserve and share these insights.

Why leadership and fishing? The common line that ties them together is human relationships. Since the beginning, there has been a vital interdependence between people and the environment. As people moved from place to place, a natural route of travel was along rivers, lakes, and oceans. These routes provided access to fish and shellfish, a readily available source of food.

Fishing required cooperative behavior. The setting of nets, the building of fish traps, and the making of equipment required teamwork. There had to be a mutually dependent relationship because the survival of one person was critically dependent on others.

This relationship continues today. Bait is gathered by one team and sold by another. Yet other teams manufacture tackle, marine supplies, and equipment. There is an extended network of people working together to make fishing an enjoyable experience.

I was reminded of the importance of relationships one winter when visiting my parents in Ormond Beach, Florida. There had been a series of storms, the golf courses were wet, and we had visited most of the tourist attractions. "Would you like to go fishing?" Dad asked. "There are several day-charter boats that operate out of an inlet near New Smyrna Beach; let's see if we can book one for tomorrow." I agreed. A charter boat was available, plans were made, and we drove down Highway 1 the next morning.

Fishing wasn't spectacularly great; however, we each caught a couple of red snapper, one of the best eating fish available on Florida's East Coast. We had a great time. It was one of the few times when we both had a completely free day to talk, build a closer relationship, and enjoy each other. It was also the last time we went fishing together. Dad died of a heart attack two months later.

Do we make the most of the opportunities we have to build relationships? Dad and I missed many of these opportunities. We went hunting a couple of times, fished for a week in northern Minnesota, and went deep-sea fishing off the coast of Hawaii, but that was about all our time of relaxing together. We had been too busy to make the investment needed to build a solid relationship. The opportunity passed, and could never be recaptured. This experience prompted me to put the emphasis on relationships that you will find in this book.

Fishing involves critical relationships such as the one between people and their environment. If excessive fishing had depleted the schools of snapper off New Smyrna Beach, our opportunity for food, recreation, and companionship would have been lost. Greed could have destroyed the great fishing area if the environment had not been respected. However, the environment has been preserved and families can continue to enjoy the New Smyrna fishing experience.

We, as anglers, have opportunities to build for the future. We can manage the quality of fish stocks, develop new fishing areas, and teach youngsters the thrill of fishing. We, as leaders, have parallel opportunities to build for the future. We can train future leaders, develop their skills, and share with them the thrill of leadership. We, as guardians of this earth, have additional opportunities to build for the future. We can improve our interactions with others and preserve our environment.

Your author, "The Old Angler," will narrate common sense information in thought provoking "bite" form. The bite will be triggered with a phrase that will highlight a key idea. Next, a sketch or story to improve your fishing skill will be described followed by short paragraphs of leadership wisdom. These bites will be summarized with a phase that will tie everything together and give you a catch to remember. You will also find a comprehensive glossary at the end of the book that will provide descriptions and definitions.

Before we go fishing, I want to acknowledge the many family members, friends, and colleagues who contributed to *Catching Success*.

Catching success, whether in fishing, leadership, or in relationships, requires cooperative behavior between team members and fishing companions. I am grateful for the many people who contributed their professional efforts and enthusiasm to this book:

My wife, Joan, who introduced me to the excitement of fishing in northern Minnesota and Canada and who constantly supported this book's development;

Ed Breedlove whose illustrations captured the essence of fishing, leadership, and relationship experiences;

Mary Moir, my sister-in-law, who set the theme of this book with her expressive photograph that appears on the cover;

Paul Hersey, Chairman of the Board, Center for Leadership Studies, Escondido, California, author of *The Situational Leader*, and Ken Blanchard, spiritual leader of the Ken Blanchard Companies, Escondido, California, and co-author of the best selling, *The One Minute Manager*. These friends were my mentors and honed my leadership skills as we worked together on four editions of *Management of Organizational Behavior: Leading Human Resources*, now in its eighth edition, published by Prentice-Hall.

Tawny L. Fulleros, Commercial Consultant, Aaron Phillips, artist, and the other professionals at Jostens, Visalia, California.

Friends at two great places for outdoor adventures:

Stuart and Terry Gill
Ontario Wilderness Houseboat Rental, LTD
Morson, Ontario, Canada POW 1JO
(800) 359-6199
(807) 488-5594

Dave and Sheree Swisten
Duck Bay Lodge, Lake of the Woods, Ontario, Canada
Winter: Box 18, Group 318, R.R. # 3, Selkirk, MB R1A2A8, (204) 757-2986
Summer: R.R. #1, Sleeman, Ontario, POW 1MO, (807) 488-5811

The generous folks who helped me by reviewing earlier versions of *Catching Success.*
Liz Cordero, daughter and skilled angler
Jennifer Hughes, daughter and skilled angler
Sam Anderson, Executive, Bay & Bay Transfer, and professional angler
Ron Campbell, President, Center for Leadership Studies
Steven Catz, professional angler and educator
Jerry Dotson, Certified Public Accountant
Beth Hunt Erickson, Author, *Wild Rice Cookbook*
Don Erickson, President, Holiday Stationstores
Jim Kalkofen, Executive Director, Professional Walleye Trail (PWT)
Bufe Karraker, Senior Pastor, Northwest Church
Daryle Lamonica, President, Mad Bomber, Inc. Tackle Company
John Lattin, President, Northwest Medical Center
Claude Laval, President, Claude Laval Corporation
Wes Moir, brother-in-law and great fishing companion

George Palmer, brother-in-law
David Shafer, Senior Management Editor, Prentice Hall Publishing
Perry Smith, muskie angler and great fishing companion
Tom Weise, Professor of Communication
Todd Valeri, General Manager, American Ambulance Company, Inc.

There were many other friends who assisted in the production of this book including Stella Bohigian, Jackie Crockett, Deb Keets, and Lisa Walzem.

Let's go fishing!

Catching Success

Ice fishing in frigid weather on a frozen river requires dedication for "catching success."

Catching Success

Fishing, leadership, and relationships are very much alike; they are filled with uncertainties.

Take fishing for example. Frank, my father-in-law, and I once spent ten hours a day for three days ice fishing on a river in northern Minnesota. We did not get a single bite. It was as cold as 35 degrees below zero; ice fog was in the air, and there were circular, hazy "sundogs" around the sun. We were dressed in arctic wear, but it was freezing cold out on the ice as the illustration shows. There was no way to haul a shelter to the fishing area over or through the ice ridges that had been pushed up by the shifting winds and the expanding and contracting ice. The only way to keep warm and to keep hope alive was to use a hand-held ice auger to make a series of fishing holes.

We tried several different techniques and types of bait-grubs, worms, minnows, jigs, lures-but they all failed. Our results were the same for the three consecutive days that we made the trip from town out to the river and back. Finally, on the morning of the fourth day, we caught six nice walleyes and went home with enough fish for a dinner for the family. Why did we persist in going back on the ice day-after-day? It was because we knew we would catch fish at that location; it was a matter of dedication and determination.

Today's fish are faced with much more fishing pressure as anglers compete for fewer, larger fish. Fishing has become a sophisticated sport with techniques and equipment unheard of just a few years ago. There are electronic fishfinders, lake maps in three dimensions, underwater optical devices, and greatly improved fishing techniques. However, there are many days when the fish are not "on bite." Does this mean your fishing trip was unsuccessful?

Not necessarily. It depends on how you define success and only you, in the final analysis, can define success. As a friend, Jason Young, suggested to me, "How do you like your steak?" I replied, "I like it medium on the few occasions when I have steak." Jason responded, "I like it medium-rare." We both say it is done when it is cooked the way we like it-medium or medium-rare.

Were the three days that Frank and I spent on the ice without catching fish unsuccessful? If we had evaluated the three days in terms of how many fish we caught, probably, yes. However, if our criterion was building a closer relationship, the three days were very, very successful.

Leadership is similar. One can attempt to lead, but until someone follows, there is no leadership. Attempted leadership, like attempted fishing is just that, attempted. A result has to be achieved for leadership to be successful. There is no leadership without followers being influenced just as there is no catching without fish. Like fishing, there are some days when even your best leadership efforts are just not enough. When people decide not to follow, there is no leadership.

Relationships are also similar. There is no guarantee that one's attempt to establish a long-term personal relationship will be successful. Again, wanting to be successful is not enough to be successful in fishing, leadership, or in relationships. All three require setting a goal, dedicating oneself to that goal, and persisting through obstacles until it is achieved or you are personally convinced it is unrealistic.

Perhaps you share Ralph Waldo Emerson's definition of success in, *How Do You Measure Success?*

> To laugh often and much;
> To win respect of intelligent people
> and the affection of children;
> To earn the appreciation of honest critics
> and endure the betrayal of false friends;
> To appreciate beauty;
> To leave the world a little better,
> Whether by a healthy child, a garden patch,
> A redeemed social condition, or a job well done;
> To know when one other life has
> breathed easier because you lived;
> This is to have succeeded.

In the final analysis, you are the only person who can define success in fishing, leadership, and relationships . . . the Old Angler's wisdom of the real definition of "catching success."

The lure will be removed without injuring the fish and a trophy bass will be released to catch another day.

Searching For
The Big One

Should you fish for that trophy bass or be grateful to catch anything that grabs your hook? You may, of course, get lucky and catch a trophy fish as many have done without trying, but fishing for "the big one" means paying very careful attention to the details.

A few anglers have caught trophy bass in Lake Castaic, north of Los Angeles, California, by using very special lures and techniques. They fish specifically with the purpose of catching largemouth bass weighing over sixteen pounds. They catch very few of these fish in relation to the number of hours they spend fishing, but the ones they catch are huge. These anglers spend an amazing number of hours perfecting their lures and techniques and even a more incredible amount of time actually fishing.

Success is in the details. It is the precise identification of habitat, the presentation of the lure, the hookup, and the reeling in. Everything has to be near perfect to land the "big one." When responsible anglers catch a large bass, they handle it very carefully as shown in the illustration. The lure is removed without injuring the bass and the fish is released. Let someone else have the enjoyment you just experienced.

We all have read the phrase, "The harder I work, the luckier I become." Fishing seemed to be so much simpler years ago. Equipment was just a cane pole, a bobber, and a simple bait hook.

Today, it seems as if you are not really prepared to fish until the weight of the gear equals the weight of your boat! Does fishing really have to be this complicated? Perhaps. There is more fishing pressure. It takes better equipment and better techniques to achieve the same cane pole level of fishing in the past.

The same point is true for leadership. Leader behavior is caused by the interaction between the leader and the situation. Leaders are not alone. Leaders swim in an ocean of competing external forces buffeted by changing economic, political, social, technical, and ecological conditions. They also are affected by their own wants and needs.

There is another related question. Should you fish to catch "the big one" or some of "the nice-eating size?" It depends upon your purpose for fishing. Why is this important? If you are fishing for the "big one" for a nice fish dinner, you have a couple of problems. One is that the largest fish are not the best eating and second, the odds of catching a big one are slim and you will go hungry most of the time. However, if your values compel you to fish for the trophy of a lifetime, then go for it but realize that an enormous amount of dedication, commitment, and luck will be required.

Leadership offers the same decision challenges when you chose between going for home runs or singles. Should you focus your organization on that once in a lifetime opportunity to capture a critical percentage of market share, a revolutionary new product, or a merger that will create new business synergies?

Going for the home run is part of the potential achievement; you have to run and touch all of the bases. As many ecommerce companies have discovered to their distress, advertising is the easy part; fulfillment, getting the goods to the customers, is the tough part.

Experience suggests that the bigger the goal, the more important it is to handle the small details. Why? The expectations are greater. When you state that you will hit one over the center field fence, your swing, the pitch, the weather, wind conditions, and many other elements have to work in perfect synchronization.

The same is true in leadership. When you set challenging goals for individuals and organizations, many, many details have to work in harmony to achieve success. This is the paradox of high achievement: bigger means smaller. Bigger fish mean more attention to the smallest details. Bigger individual and organizational achievements mean more attention to the many small steps that contribute to effective performance.

Paying attention to the details increases the probability of catching the trophy fish . . . the Old Angler's wisdom of searching for the big one.

The mouth of Duck Bay inlet offers great fishing after several days of high winds.

Fish Where The Fish Are Running

You have arrived at a lake where you have never fished before. You have, however, spent some time examining the contour lines of the lake's topographical chart. Your object is to look for possible fish-holding structures such as breaklines, reefs, humps, and points. You also look for potential currents.

In many larger lakes, if the wind blows steadily in one direction for several days, the water level builds up on the windswept shore. When the wind decreases, the water seeks its natural level creating significant currents between islands and around points.

The photograph on the cover was taken at sunset from Duck Bay Lodge in Sabaskong Bay in Lake of the Woods. My brother-in-law, Wes Moir, and I decided to go out fishing after dinner. We were fishing just outside the resort where there is an inlet leading into a small bay and a large marsh.

The wind had calmed after blowing for several days and baitfish in the marsh were leaving to go into the larger Sabaskong Bay. Walleyes, northerns, and muskies were patrolling just outside the inlet looking for a meal and we were searching for these game fish.

Weather conditions directed us to the mouth of the inlet. However, as you look over an expanse of water, you must remind yourself that only about 10 percent of the lake has a good probability of holding fish. You need to fish where the fish are and this takes study and preparation.

Joan, my wife, and her sister, Mary Moir, had decided to stay on shore and linger over coffee by the big fireplace in the lodge's dining room. After awhile, they wondered how we were doing and walked down to the shore to observe. Mary snapped the cover photograph of this tranquil scene.

A successful business executive was asked to share what she believed to be a fundamental business principle. She replied, "Fish where the fish are running." I asked what she meant. She replied, "Put your resources where they have the best opportunity for success."

She went on to explain that her corporation practices target marketing by using rather sophisticated techniques to find those persons most likely to buy. The corporation then puts marketing efforts toward those potential customers.

The firm also works hard to retain existing customers because their retention costs are much lower than the costs of developing new customers.

Bo Gyllenpalm, an internationally known consultant from Sweden, relates this idea to leadership. He suggests that people have limited energy and must focus this energy where it counts. He uses the analogy of the sun's rays. Unfocused rays can't start a fire; focused rays using a magnifying glass can easily start a fire.

Leaders must use the magnifying glass of purpose to focus their limited energy.

You must ask, "What do I want to accomplish and where is the best place to accomplish this purpose?" These simple questions remove from consideration 90 percent of the "lake" and enable you to vastly increase your probability of success.

Focus your leadership efforts . . . the Old Angler's wisdom of fish where the fish are running.

A channel just a short distance from Mary Ester, Florida, provides access to the Gulf of Mexico.

The Channel

Our family likes to go fishing for king mackerel off the North Florida coast in the Gulf of Mexico. King mackerel, also known as kingfish, are bright silver with a small dorsal fin. We have caught "kings" weighing as much as forty-five pounds, but our average catch is about fifteen pounds.

The Gulf's water conditions are smooth for the family's 19' Bayliner most of the year, but the prevailing winds and swells make going through the channel from our favorite marina to the Gulf very challenging.

The channel that we frequently use to enter the Gulf of Mexico is about two hundred feet wide and as the waves roll into the channel, they bounce off the rock breakwaters lining the channel and increase in size. Two-foot waves in the Gulf become five-foot waves in the channel.

However, this is only part of the problem. As the waves collide with the rocks, they rebound back into the channel and bounce off other waves creating wave patterns from several directions. In addition, the wake from boats entering and leaving the channel churns up the water.

The family's safety is primary. Before we enter the channel, we put on and check our life jackets, make sure all of the navigation lights are working, and prepare throw ropes and float cushions ready to use. It was pretty scary the first time we entered the channel and we were apprehensive. It was a new experience, but we were prepared for the challenges and were motivated by the relatively calm water beyond the breakwater and thoughts of hooking big kingfish.

A new leadership position is much like this channel. A person in the first few days of a new leadership position is faced with many cross-currents: "waves" left from former holders of that position, attitudes (swells) from previous experience, and constraints (breakwaters) caused by the organizational structure and culture. All of these forces create a turbulent environment during a person's first few days at work.

It is easy to make mistakes and to be capsized by unseen forces. What amplifies the problem is that you go into this position with a relatively clean experience record. People may not know very much about your previous boat-handling achievements and, perhaps, the few barnacles you have acquired.

Therefore, your mistakes are magnified. There is just not enough evidence to make a balanced picture. You must wear a "life jacket" of awareness and be prepared, right from the start, to always produce something extra.

For example, operate on Vince Lombardi time. Vince was the award winning coach of the Green Bay Packers professional football team when they won the first two Super Bowl Championships. He used to say, "If you are fifteen minutes early, you are fifteen minutes late."

Leaders and anglers face similar challenging situations; a narrow channel creates difficult water conditions where errors are compounded. You have to use all of your skills and experience to pilot a successful route through the maelstrom into the bay's calmer water.

Wear a life jacket!

Prepare for challenges when you start a new leadership position . . . the Old Angler's wisdom of the channel.

A fishing tournament board before the action starts. Who will win the top prize?

The Best Don't Always Finish First

Many highly skilled anglers participate in fishing competitions such as the In-Fisherman Professional Walleye Trail or B.A.S.S. tournaments. The leader board is a popular attraction during the competition. There is usually a large crowd of spectators and anglers who have completed their day's competition gathered by the leader board.

After the tournament is over, the sponsoring organization publishes a list of each competitor's standing or rank order. Anglers who placed high or even won a tournament might not finish in the top 75 percent in the next tournament. Have they lost their skills? Probably not. The main reason for skilled anglers finishing high in one tournament and much lower in another is that there are many variables affecting fishing success.

What may work in one fishing situation may not work in another and, in fact, may be counterproductive. For example, jigging with a leech may be the best technique, trolling with a minnow or worm, or casting crankbaits may all be productive techniques sometimes, but not every time. Wind, water conditions, type of underwater structures, and luck are some of the variables affecting fishing success.

The illustration on the facing page represents the leader board of a fishing tournament. There are no names because the final list of professional competitors and their amateur partners is still being compiled. There are no weights of the fish caught, and later released, because the competition is hours away from starting. Who will win prizes? No one knows. It cannot be predicted. Results of past tournaments indicate that even the anglers who have been named "Angler of the Year" in the past may finish near the bottom of the list this time.

Leadership, because it involves the infinite variables of people and their situations, may not always result in success. What works in one situation probably will not work in another. You, as a leader, might want to achieve success in every leadership intervention, but you probably will not because of circumstances beyond your control.

Think of almost any area of human endeavor. Can you name musicians who have been consistently successful throughout their music careers? Can you recall business leaders who have been successful in every firm they have led? Do you know many politicians who have won every election? It is very, very difficult to find individuals or organizations with perfect records. We all have our times of achievement and other times where we did not do as well as we expected. It goes with being an angler, a leader, or in a relationship.

Skilled and experienced leaders do not always achieve success . . . the Old Angler's wisdom of the best don't always finish first.

Catching Success

Through Leadership

Selecting the right fly increases the opportunity for successful trout fishing.

Matching The Hatch

John Lattin, one of my best friends, taught me a key element of fly fishing-matching the hatch-in other words selecting an artificial fly that would match the natural insects that were hatching and rising from the water's surface. John had learned to fly fish in the mountains of Utah and had many years of experience. John demonstrated how important it was to select a hook with the right shape. He also taught me how to tie a fly with bits of feather and other materials such as deer hair and colored thread to resemble a natural insect.

John explained that there were many standard flies that could be bought to match the seasonal hatch, but it was important to learn how to tie flies to match special conditions or to replace flies that had been lost or damaged. Using the wrong fly would mean little or no success; using the best match would increase the probability of success.

I have learned to use several different wet and dry flies. Wet flies are designed to sink beneath the surface and imitate food that is suspended in the water or is on the bottom. Wet flies are very effective because about 80 percent of the food is beneath the surface. Dry flies are designed to imitate surface insects. I was soon able to use certain favorites such as the Gold-Ribbed Hare's Ear, Woolly Bugger, Griffith's Gnat, and the Gray Wulff shown in the illustration on the facing page.

My first choice when I would go fly-fishing would be one of my favorite flies. Sometimes, however, my favorites were not very successful. They didn't match the hatch.

The same principle applies to crankbait casting; the lure has to match the forage, what the fish are eating. Crankbaits are lures that are used for casting or trolling. In the spring, baitfish are smaller and the appropriate choice is a small lure. Then, as the baitfish grow larger, the angler should match the forage by increasing the size of the lure.

Live bait selection should also change. If you are using live bait fishing for walleyes, perhaps minnows are the appropriate bait for spring and fall fishing while worms are the best in the summer.

The same approach can be applied to fly fishing in a stream. One type of fly will work in one situation, but not in another. The same idea is true when fishing crankbaits. One size of lure will work in one situation, but not in another. The fish will dictate what will trigger them.

Matching the hatch also applies to leadership. The leader must assess how prepared people, individually or in a team, are to be led. This means looking at the personal and organizational conditions in a given situation. Is more direction and control necessary or is a team ready to run with the ball and receive very little guidance? Does a team have experience in performing the task or does it need counseling, guidance, and perhaps some motivation?

Very different leadership styles or approaches are needed for individuals or teams at different levels of readiness. Readiness means having the ability to do the task and the motivation to do it.

The term readiness comes from the children's game of "Hide and Seek." Do you remember running to hide while the "finder" counted to fifty and then called out, "Here I come . . . ready or not?" If you were new to the game and had difficulty finding a good hiding place, you would be caught rather easily and might need detailed instructions before playing the next game. You were "not ready" to have a high probability of "catching success" by avoiding being found.

If you were an experienced player, you probably were highly motivated and skilled at finding an excellent hiding place. You did not need very much, if any, direction or encouragement. You were "ready" to really play the game with a high probability of success.

If an individual or team has performed a task successfully many times and has the motivation to continue to do it well, little direction and encouragement is needed. However, if the task is new to an individual or team, then more instruction and guidance are needed. This is a straightforward issue. What will work with one individual or team will probably not work with another. In fishing terms, your leadership style must "match the hatch."

Lead in response to individual and team readiness . . . the Old Angler's wisdom of matching the hatch.

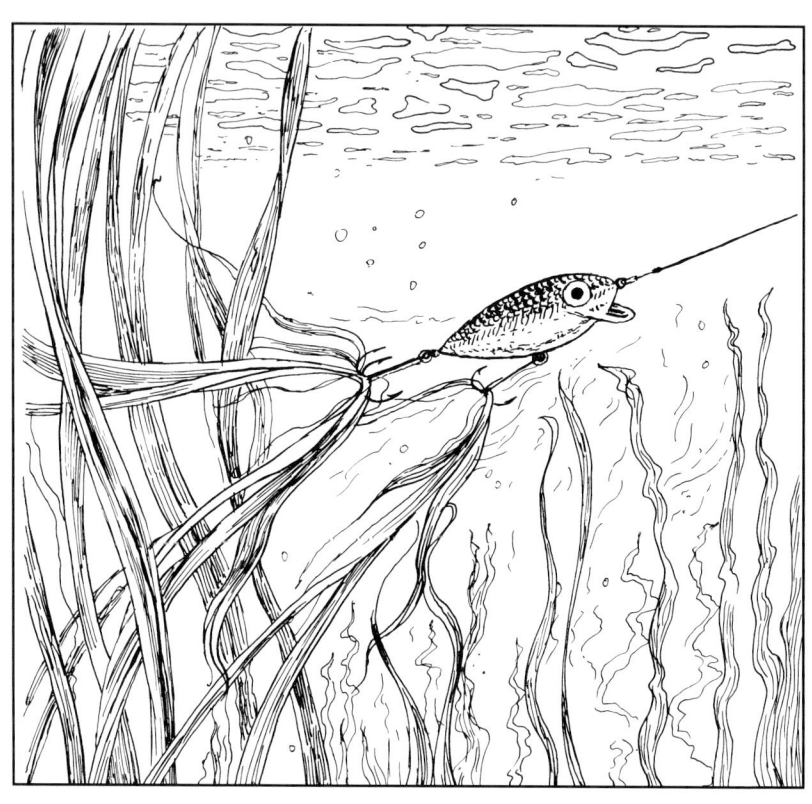

A lure catching weeds will not catch many fish.

Clean The Weeds

You are trolling for trout. After a while, you wonder why you haven't had any strikes. Your companion says, "Better check for weeds." You reel in your lure and see that there are small pieces of weeds on your hooks; not many, but it takes only one to keep the fish from biting.

Weeds are a special problem when you are fishing in or close to weed beds - but you have no choice. This is where the fish are feeding at certain times of the year and if you are going to enjoy some success, you are going to catch weeds.

Leaders may pick up weeds that keep them from reaching their potential. Morgan W. McCall, Jr., Michael M. Lombardo, Ann M. Morrison, and Robert W. Eichinger, prominent leadership researchers and authors, have identified several of these leadership "weeds":

- Insensitivity to others: abrasive, intimidating, bullying style
- Cold, aloof, arrogant
- Untrustworthy
- Overly ambitious: always thinking of the next job, playing politics
- Unable to delegate or build a team – overmanaging
- Unable to think strategically
- Unable to adapt to a boss with a different style

The potential for acquiring these weeds exists in almost every organization. Therefore, leaders must be alert to them even if they think they are using so-called weedless lures. Leaders should remember that it is the perception of others that counts, not their personal perceptions.

This important idea is discussed in Paul Hersey's *The Situational Leader*. Paul uses a phrase that summarizes the fundamental concept of perception. "All of our behavior is evoked by our perceptions and interpretations of reality."

What one perceives . . . is actually reality. Seeing is truly believing.

Image that you are walking through woods and you stumble over a stick, but you perceive it to be a snake. How do you react? You walk further through the woods and you step on a snake, but you perceive it to be a stick and continue walking until the snake strikes and bites you.

What you don't perceive can frequently turn around and bite you!

Leaders have to be constantly on the alert for weeds that can snag them and drag them down. How can leaders prevent catching weeds?

Fishing provides some clues. Anglers can use hooks that have their barbs covered so they do not snag weeds. They can use techniques such as reeling in as soon as the lure lands in the water. They can search for select open areas to place their casts.

Leaders can use similar behaviors. They can take more care in working with people. It is not necessary to use sharp "word barbs" to get people's attention. Leaders can give followers the information they need right away without holding it back to play "got you." They can select key areas to delegate.

How do these approaches apply to relationships? Perhaps in the same way they apply to fishing and leadership: care in what you say, openness in communication, and sharing of responsibilities.

If you have ever had a sharp hook caught in your hand, you know it hurts. The only way to remove it without considerable pain is to cut off the barb. The hook can then be removed relatively painlessly and without further injury. If you can not prevent weeds in leadership and relationships, cut them off as soon as possible so you can resume your interactions without further pain . . . for yourself and others.

———◆———

Be alert for behaviors that hinder your leadership . . . the Old Angler's wisdom of cleaning the weeds.

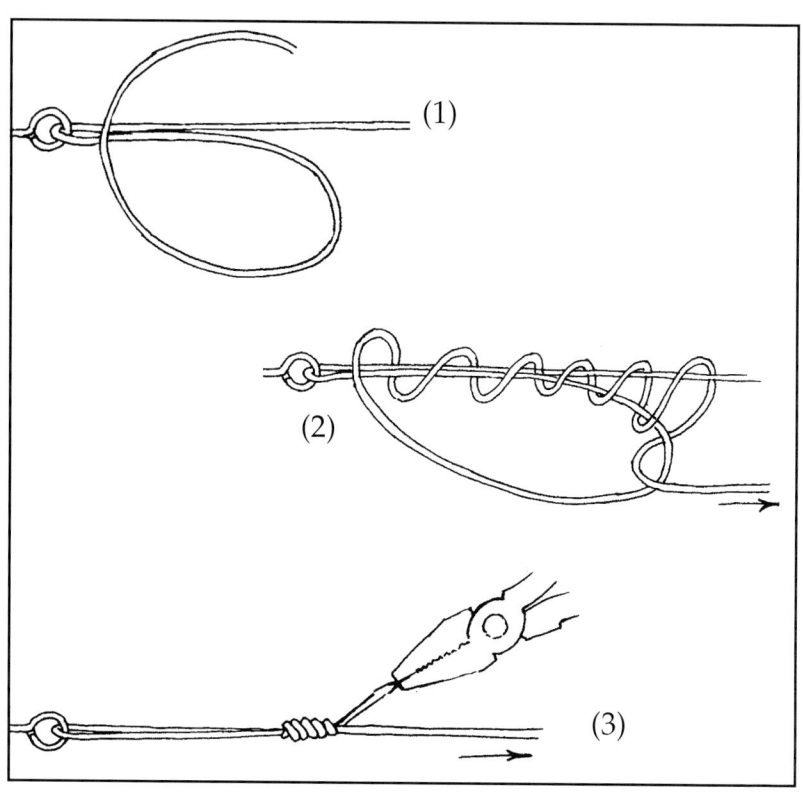

There are three easy steps to tying a loop.

Tying A Loop

Some lures such as the Rapala Shad Rap are designed to use their inherent, crafted design to create a fish-enticing action. Other lures such as jerkbaits, Texas rigs, Carolina rigs, and jigs are designed to be maneuvered by the angler who controls the presentation. However, even lures such as the Shad Rap do not maneuver themselves. The angler controls the speed of the retrieve, decides where the lure is cast or trolled, and selects the size and type of lure.

However, the Shad Rap, like many other types of lures, is not designed to be fished with a leader made from wire, monofilament line, or braided line. A leader restricts the movement that is designed into the lure. The angler should not tie a fishing line or fasten a leader directly to the lure because this also restricts movement. The lure will not perform as it should.

Through much practice, trial and error, and coaching from more experienced anglers, I have learned to tie a loop so the lure can perform its designed action. There are several ways that this loop can be tied, but one of my favorites is the uni-knot illustrated on the facing page. The advantage of this knot is that it retains almost 100 percent of the line strength when under a steady pull or even when a monster fish jerks it.

The illustration shows an uni-knot being tied to a lure

such as a crankbait. There are three steps to this process:

1. The fishing line is threaded through the lure's eyelet and brought back and around in a loop.

2. The free end of the line is then wrapped around the two strands of the line. Four to five wraps are enough when you are using a heavy line such as a monofilament line greater than ten-pound test. Two or three more wraps are required when you are using a lighter test line.

3. The knot is moistened and drawn tight with a pair of pliers. This will give a loop that will take advantage of the lure's natural fish-catching movement plus a strong knot that will not harm your spirit by breaking at a critical time.

If you are tying the line directly to a swivel, for example, you do not need a loop. You can moisten the knot, slide the knot down to the swivel, snug it against the swivel and pull both the line and the swivel to secure the knot. How does this apply to leadership?

Micromanaging leaders hold tightly to their followers. They may use a leadership style that is so restrictive that followers have little freedom to use their talents. Followers may be so controlled that the leader restricts their every movement.

Leadership is much like catch and release fishing. You must liberate people to let them develop. Fish can't grow in a live well, a small, restrictive compartment in a boat that is used to keep fish alive. People can't grow and develop under close, restrictive supervision. Leaders have to contribute to the personal growth of their followers by encouraging, providing opportunities, and releasing their followers to reach their potential.

There are, however, situations where even experienced followers require tight control when performing tasks of high risk to themselves and/or to others. For example, when a team of fire fighters is searching a burning building, they must follow very precise procedures for their safety. However, fire fighting is not the usual leadership situation.

The more common situation that leaders face is when they have teams of experienced people. These employees know what to do and how to do it. If given freedom, they will perform their jobs. The problem occurs when micromanaging is used inappropriately with followers who are already highly motivated. The leader should cut them some slack and give them room to maneuver, just as anglers give certain lures a free rein. A tight rein reduces their performance. They do not need restricting leaders.

Let your experienced followers perform freely . . . the Old Angler's wisdom of tying a loop.

Several different crankbaits are used for walleye fishing.

Too Much Plastic

I fished as an amateur in a Professional Walleye Trail tournament at Devil's Lake, North Dakota, that included five days of practice fishing to assess the lake conditions and three days of competitive fishing. There was one section of the lake that offered great potential because there was about twenty feet of water over a marsh that was flooded when the lake rose.

Fishing regulations allowed each angler to use two lines. With two anglers in each boat and more than two hundred boats on the lake including competitors and local anglers, the fish saw thousands of lure presentations in this area.

The anglers trolled similar crankbaits at similar depths for eight to twelve hours a day for eight days. Many fish were caught and released and they became sensitized to the lures. As a result, fishing over these flats declined each day until it was very difficult to catch any fish. On the third day of the tournament, only a few anglers tried this area and most were unsuccessful.

As one professional angler observed, "The fish saw too much plastic!"

The anglers who were successful in this tournament went back to a simple monofilament line, no spinner or beads, and a hook baited with a leech fished in traditional fish-holding holes. They did not troll the same old stuff; they adapted to the basic needs of the fish. These anglers offered simple presentation to appeal to the fish's basic needs.

Have your employees seen too much plastic? Have they seen the same programs used over and over again in an attempt to motivate them? In many organizations, the same incentive programs are trolled past people time and time again. Perhaps it is time to get down to basics.

What are some of these basics?

An example from Pelco, the world leader in video security equipment and systems, based in Clovis, California, illustrates these basics. Pelco employees gather toys for the annual Toys for Tots campaign and the company matches their donations. Their 1999 total was 74,000 toys, an amazing accomplishment.

The employees more than doubled their 1999 results in 2000 and Pelco matched them for a total of 149,408 toys, perhaps the largest single contribution in the fifty-two year history of Toys For Tots. What an achievement – doubling an amazing effort in just one year!

The *Fresno Bee* reported the many factors that made this singular feat happen:

Passion and dedication – Everyone worked on this project throughout the year.

Focus - Toys for needy children needed to be collected

before December 25.

Teamwork – Employees were organized into teams; there was teamwork between employees and management.

Creativity – New and innovative ways of raising funds were required to double the number of toys.

Leadership – Pelco matched toys the employees collected.

Celebration – A Marine white-gloved salute, marching band, color guard, Santas carried by helicopters, all contributed to a special celebration.

Some companies recycle plastic; Pelco and its employees create golden moments for themselves and 150,000 children!

Focus on the basics . . . the Old Angler's wisdom of too much plastic.

Carving a figure 8 with your rod tip in the water will often trigger a muskie to bite.

The "Muskie 8" Technique

Muskie fishing is very difficult and, as a result, there are many new techniques to learn. The muskellunge or muskie is one of the great freshwater game fish, a strong, solitary, and a challenging fighter. In Ontario, Canada, for example, the minimum legal length is 34 to 48 inches. In most of the fifty states, the minimum legal length is usually over thirty inches.

One of the proven fishing techniques is the "Muskie 8." You take your fishing rod, plunge the tip into the water by your boat, and cut a couple of figure 8s in the water with your rod tip before lifting your lure on board. The reason for doing this is that muskies like to follow a lure, frequently unseen by the angler. They will strike the lure just as it reaches the boat, particularly if it is swept around in a figure 8 pattern.

It works like this. You select a likely spot, perhaps a rock shelf dropping off into deep water with some weed cover or a narrow gap between two islands. You look for a place where a muskie can patrol while searching for a prospective meal, usually a walleye, sucker, or perch. Muskies will attack almost anything that they can eat including small mammals, ducklings, and even other muskies.

You use a two-handed cast and retrieve your bucktail jerkbait or crankbait fast enough so the lure stays a couple of feet below the surface and retains its designed movement. Perhaps you see a swirl or even a long dark shape following your lure. The fish doesn't strike, but you hope that it will. You may want to increase or decrease the speed of the retrieve or jerk the lure from side to side to trigger the muskie to strike.

Now you are reeling your lure close to the boat. You sense that a muskie is ready to strike. You put your rod tip into the water, start to make a figure 8 with your bucktail just below the surface and just as you make the first curve of your figure 8, a muskie strikes.

WOW!

You are about to experience one of the greatest thrills in fishing, playing and landing one of the giant fresh-water fish. If you catch one, you have to handle it carefully because muskies tire quickly and are easily injured. The technique that best prevents injury is to use a cradle - two pieces of wood supporting a finely woven net or canvas bottom. The muskie is eased onto a cradle where you can remove the lure and release the fish. You don't need a trophy; let it go and let another angler have some fun.

Leadership, like muskie fishing, is hard work. You first need to select the objective you want to achieve. It means concentrating on this objective and assessing people you are attempting to lead to determine if they can carry out the defined objective. Then, having made this assessment, you need to lead until the objective is reached. In other words, practice doing the muskie 8.

You don't stop leadership after a short period of time . . . muskies are not going to jump into your boat after a few turns of the reel! One must remember that landing a trophy muskie can take about 10,000 casts.

The same type of effort is required for leadership. People are not going to be influenced with a few casual words. You need to complete the process. This means monitoring progress along the way, watching for times when you need to encourage, looking for times when you need to provide more direction. Just as in fishing, you learn to lead by receiving sound advice and practicing proven techniques. You must continue the leadership process until the objective is reached.

Lead until the process is completed . . . the Old Angler's wisdom of remembering the "muskie 8."

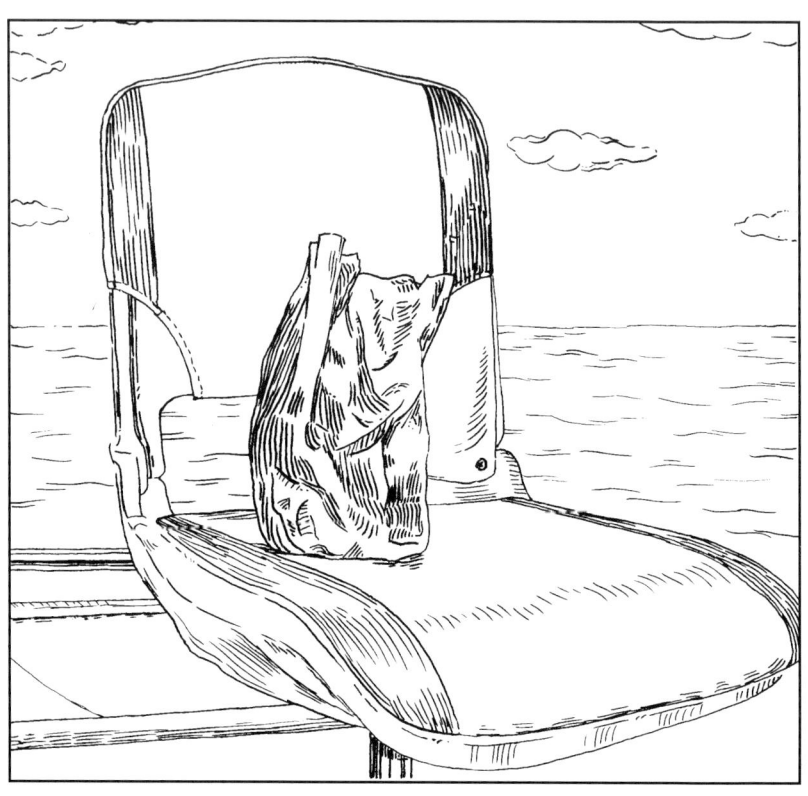

A paper bag "tackle box" on an angler's fishing chair is waiting for the action to begin.

Your Tackle Box Is A Paper Bag

Steve Catz, an angler who fishes on the B.A.S.S. tournament trail, joined me for breakfast one morning. While we were waiting for coffee and menus, Steve asked me to name the four lures I would put in a paper bag to use for largemouth bass fishing that would cover depths from top water down to twenty feet. What four would give me the most flexibility?

I named four for my "paper bag" tackle box and Steve told me my selections were good, but did not cover a wide enough range of conditions and depths. He suggested the following and gave me some reasons why:

Surface To Two Feet. A one-half ounce spinnerbait complete with a white head and a white, chartreuse, and blue skirt. The blade would be a single hammered-copper Colorado blade. The hook could be tipped with a piece of worm or pork to make it more weedless and to add to the attraction. The depth would be controlled by the speed of the retrieve.

Two to Five feet. A number 5 Rapala Shad Rap perch style (deep running). This is one of the most flexible lures. I have caught and released large- and smallmouth bass, northern pike, walleyes, and muskies on this lure.

Five to Ten Feet. A one-half ounce chrome bottom/blue

back Bill Norman Rattle Trap crankbait. The depth is controlled by the speed of the retrieve.

Zero to Twenty Feet. A one-half ounce "pig 'n jig." Black jig head ("jig") with a black and blue skirt. You can use a black Zoom Super Chunk ("pig") as a trailer. This lure is fished using a pitching or flipping technique. You take out the slack and retrieve it very slowly letting the lure swim near the bottom.

Before you start making phone calls and sending letters and e-mail to remind me of others, please be assured that these are only representative lures. You may agree with Steve or have other personal favorites. I am partial to a spinner bait with a chartreuse Colorado blade and skirt.

There are just as many leadership styles or behaviors as there are fishing lures. In order to put only four styles in our leadership "paper bag," I have chosen the four basic styles explained in the eighth edition of *Management of Organizational Behavior: Leading Human Resources,* by Paul Hersey, Ken Blanchard, and Dewey Johnson.

Style 1. The leader provides specific instructions and closely supervises the followers' performances.

Style 2. The leader explains the task to be performed and provides opportunity for the followers to ask questions for clarification.

Style 3. The leader shares ideas with followers and facilitates in the decision making process.

Style 4. The leader turns over responsibility for decision making and implementation while monitoring performance.

Just as with fishing lures, there are many, many variations on these leadership behaviors. As we have noted before, the leadership style and fishing lure/technique that you use depends on the environment. If it is summer and bass are deep, then you may wish to use a centipede instead of a lizard on your Carolina rig and fish it very slowly.

If your followers are very experienced in and motivated toward a task, you may wish to use Style 4 with less directing and supporting behavior. What you want to do and how ready your finny friends or your followers are to do it dictate your approach as you reach in your paper bag for one of your four lures or select from your inventory of four basic leadership styles.

Build on fundamental fishing techniques and leadership styles . . . the Old Angler's wisdom of your tackle box is a paper bag.

A backyard pool is a great place to test equipment and techniques.

The Practice Pool

One morning, Daryle Lamonica, formerly of the National Football League's Oakland Raiders and one of the league's all-time great quarterbacks, invited me over to his house to look at some fishing tackle he had designed for his company, Mad-Bomber, Inc. I found Daryle practicing with a lure in his backyard swimming pool.

I naturally asked him what he was doing. "Checking out the action and presentation of my lures before going to the lake," was Daryle's response. I watched Daryle try out different lures, making some adjustments to make them run true, changing the speed of the retrieve of others, all to make sure that the different lures were finely tuned.

One lure kept moving to the left. He retrieved the lure and using a pair of needle nose pliers, bent the eyelet slightly to the left. He tested this adjustment a couple of times and then selected another lure.

This was a "countdown or jerkbait" lure that sinks at a predictable rate. The technique is to cast the lure, count as it sinks, and when it has reached the desired depth you give it short jerks to make the lure dart back and forth with a slow retrieve. This lure was sinking at too slow a rate so he added very small weight dots to increase the sink rate. Daryle then tested this and also checked the lure's balance.

We tested different plastic baits such as tubes, grubs, worms, lizards and craws. We rigged dart heads, Texas rigs, Carolina rigs, and top water lures to observe their performance. The backyard pool was perfect because we could observe what was happening in the crystal clear water.

Daryle believes that you can catch more fish if you can visualize exactly what your lure is doing under water.

Where can leaders practice? Where are their practice pools where they can test performance? Figuratively, they can be in their own back yards. Just as one can fish in a small farm pond, leaders can hone their skills in their day-to-day interactions.

Leadership, as defined in this book, can occur wherever there is potential interaction among people, individually or in teams. You can practice leadership skills in your family, in social situations, or in community organizations; there is always a potential to influence.

You do not have to wait for a formal organizational setting.

You can also hone your skills in many different ways: by participating in seminars and workshops, receiving coaching and mentoring, and accepting new challenges and responsibilities.

Tournament contestants use a period before the competition starts to investigate the body of water where they will be competing. It is called "practice fishing," but it is really fishing.

The same idea can be applied to leadership; you need to practice so you can excel in performance situations. It is frequently too late when the fish are biting to fine tune your equipment, hone your skills, and sharpen your hooks.

Practice and test before performing ... the Old Angler's wisdom of the practice pool.

Who caught this walleye mounted on a driftwood plaque in a hometown restaurant?

Fish Can't Tell The Gender

Two couples had fun staging an informal three-day fishing tournament. The rules were catch and release. As soon as the species could be identified, it was counted as caught. No fish were brought into the boat. Points were assigned for each identifiable fish hooked; perch did not count.

Who had the highest point total? One of the men or one of the women? The champion after three days was one of the ladies. Fish don't know the gender of the angler. It is individual skill, knowledge, and a little bit of luck that counts. Men and women have become highly skilled anglers.

It is just like the mounted walleye in the illustration. There is no way of telling if a woman or a man caught it.

The same is true in leadership. Both genders have excelled as leaders. In fact, men and women leaders are more alike in their leadership skills than are women and men in the general population. There are many current writings about women having better leadership skills in some situations, while men have better leadership skills in other situations.

For example, it has been suggested that women are more effective leaders when a participative leadership style is indicated. A typical situation calling for this style is when team members need to mutually decide an important issue. Focused discussion and consideration for other team members may be necessary.

It has also been suggested that men may be more effective leaders in crisis situations where immediate decisions have to be made. A typical situation calling for this style is a response to a competitor's pricing changes. Your competitor has raised its prices on certain product lines by 5 percent. Do you match this increase? Your market and your other competitors are waiting for you to act.

Research has shown that most effective leaders, regardless of gender, share similar attributes. Some women may be more effective in situations calling for teamwork, but so are some men. Some men may be more effective in situations calling for decisive decision making, but so are some women.

The key point is how effective a person, regardless of gender, can be as a leader. It is a question of influence. In every situation, there are ways of influencing an individual or team to achieve results.

Perhaps it is a situation that requires the leader to have expertise in consensus-building, working with a team to reach agreement on a course of action. Consensus-building relies on skill of the facilitator, knowledge of techniques, and experience in helping with the process. Effectiveness in this situation is an ability issue, not a gender issue.

One of the problems in assessing leadership effectiveness is that leaders have several roles. One of these roles is that leaders may have to perform technical tasks. For example, a movie director may have to design adjustments in the lighting of a set, placing of cameras, or staging of the action. These actions are products of the director's technical expertise.

Once the director has made these design decisions, leadership is required to influence people to execute them. For example, the movie director must influence a crew to make the necessary lighting adjustments.

Men and women can have the requisite technical as well as leadership ability.

There is no best gender-specific leadership situation.

A fish doesn't know the gender of the person holding the pole; it is either triggered to bite or not. Followers, in the final analysis, are either influenced or not.

Both men and women can be effective leaders ... the Old Angler's wisdom of fish can't tell the gender.

An Indian pictograph was painted long ago on a rock wall near the entrance to Turtle Portage in Ontario, Canada.

Learning From The Kids

I decided to hire a guide to fish for largemouth bass. Although I had fished in Lake of the Woods for more than four decades and had explored almost every part of the lake, largemouth bass had never been on the fishing agenda. To be quite honest, I didn't know until a friend told me the day before that there were largemouth in the lake.

I made arrangements through a resort for a guide and was surprised when a seventeen-year-old came down to pick me up. What can this kid teach me? I knew everything about fishing. To make the situation even more complicated, the young guide had brought along a friend who was also a guide. What am I going to do with these kids? I was not very happy when we loaded our gear and left the dock.

My good nature started to return when the kids took me on a route that I had never seen before because my fishing boat could not be winched over the portage. We went through Turtle Channel, named after a painting of a turtle on a rock face that an Indian tribe had made many decades before. What an impressive sight!

We then pulled the guides' boat across Turtle Portage into Whitefish Bay. I was glad there was an extra hand along because we had to winch the boat over wooden rollers up a ten-foot high ramp, across twenty feet of wooden rollers, and then let the boat down the other side. It was very hard work even for the three of us.

The kids directed us to a narrow channel about six miles from the portage. I had seen this channel previously when coming from another direction where I did not have to portage, but it seemed so choked with water lilies that it appeared impossible to fish. With two of us taking turns using the oars to push through the vegetation, we were able to force the boat up a small, almost unseen passageway into more open water.

"How did you know about this place?" I asked my young guide.

"My grandfather showed me. We used to come here a couple of times a year," he replied.

Our plan was for one guide to run the electric trolling motor because of all the weeds. I cast lures from the forward pedestal seat and the other guide cast from the rear pedestal seat and helped in the selecting and changing of the lures.

The largemouth bass fishing was great!

We used weedless lures; the Super Prop from Mister Twister seemed to work best. We threw to the lily pads, let the lures rest on the pads for a few seconds, and then jerked them off. As soon as the lure fell off the pad, there would be a swirl of a largemouth bass strike, and frequently a catch. "These kids are good," I thought. We worked as a team and had a successful day of fishing.

Leadership teams now are the way to go. Most *Fortune 500* companies have more than half of their employees working in teams. The word *TEAM* explains it all. As suggested by Jack Parnell, media consultant to the Miller Brewing Corporation, T.E.A.M. means: Together. Everyone. Accomplishes. More.

I overcame my initial concerns and joined the team. The kids had special expertise to contribute to the team. The fishing experience was great, better than I had anticipated, and I had the opportunity to enjoy a new adventure.

Together. Everyone. Accomplishes. More. . . . the Old Angler's wisdom of learning from the kids.

The dining room of a fishing lodge with a lake in the background provides a place to plan a day of fishing.

Let The Guide, Guide

I stopped by the dining room of a fish camp for breakfast and overheard a fisherman instructing his guide for the day. "We want to start at 8:00 and fish for walleyes until we catch enough for shore lunch. This will be about 10:00 if you are any good. We then want to fish for bass until we have shore lunch at 11:45. At 1:00, we want to fish for muskies for two hours and then for northern pike from 3:00 until 4:00 when we will head back to camp."

The guide listened quietly, but his body posture reflected amazement. Why did this guest need a guide if the schedule was predetermined?

When a leader hires experienced employees, these employees should be given the freedom to do their work. You set general guidelines, but let them perform. It is the first rule of delegation. Decide if you want to delegate, what you want to delegate, and set performance expectations. Then, let your experts do their work.

Guides may have one of the most performance-driven jobs because they are expected to have enough fish for shore lunch in spite of many adverse conditions and severe time constraints.

This is a typical scenario. A guide may be responsible for up to six or even more anglers. Departure time is about

8:00 and shore lunch is normally prepared between 11:45 and 1:00. It usually takes from thirty to sixty minutes to reach the fishing area, perhaps another hour to find fish. It is now between 9:30 and 10:00.

This leaves the guide only about ninety minutes to catch two pounds of fish (live weight) per angler, reach the shore lunch spot, unload the cooking equipment, and began making preparations for the meal. Meanwhile the guests are gathering wood, repairing the fire pit, and relaxing.

This schedule will work if everything goes right, but this is not the normal situation. Adverse weather conditions may make finding and catching fish very difficult. There are other problems such as those described below:

Guests may fool around, forget equipment, have another cup of coffee, and departure time will be delayed fifteen to thirty minutes.

Guests may not know how to land fish so they lose them at the net or, even worse, knock the guide's fish off through clumsy net technique.

Guests may not know how to bait their hooks, play fish, and remove hooks.

Guests may snag the bottom and lose equipment, tangle their lines, break rods and reels, and throw equipment overboard in the excitement of landing a fish. (The Old Angler has done that!)

And the list goes on.

A most welcome sight for a guide is an experienced angler who can "captain" one of the boats by helping with the problems listed above and catching a few fish.

A most welcome sight for you should be an expert who can share your load. Guides do not like to have shore lunch at 2:00 in the afternoon.

Do you like to have to work in the evenings and on weekends because you can't or won't delegate?

If you need help, let the experts perform . . . the Old Angler's wisdom of let the guide, guide.

What a mess! Another spilled tackle box.

Sort Your Tackle Box

What a mess! One of my new plastic tackle boxes had been tipped upside down and lures and other fishing gear were all tangled. There was nothing I could do but straighten the mess. I decided this would be a good time for me to go through my other tackle boxes and sort my fishing gear into what was working and what was not.

There were several spinners that were rusted and bent and looked as if they had not been used in years and they probably hadn't. Other lures were one-time attractions; they had hooked me in the store, but they did not seem likely to attract any fish. However, there were many old standbys in the boxes such as Mepps bucktail spinners, Rapala Shad Raps, and Lindy Little Joe jigs.

The problem was that there was so much outdated and damaged gear that it was difficult to find the winners. Finally, I was able to put aside the good gear, purchase new plastic boxes, and secure the treble hooks in guards to keep them from being so easily tangled. Now it was time to go fishing.

Leaders occasionally need to clean out their leadership tool kits. For example, they need to update their language. Perhaps they have fallen into the habit of using terms and concepts that are so out-of-date that their potential followers can not relate to them. They need to find out what is working and what is not.

Leaders face many other leadership challenges: leadership in an increasingly diverse work force, training for technology, and planning for leadership succession. Yesterday's skills will not be effective in today's and tomorrow's world.

Consider that almost every profession has continuing education requirements. Accountants, nurses, attorneys, physicians, and teachers all require approved continuing education credit to maintain their licenses or certifications. However, these are just to maintain their certifications; there is other formal training they must take to improve their skills. In addition, they must read professional literature to keep up with new developments. Their education is a continuing obligation.

Leaders have an awesome responsibility. They affect people's lives. Their decisions have a tremendous impact on people both inside and outside their organizations. The way leaders handle promotions, transfers, changing job assignments, physical relocations within the office or plant, and more basically, the way people are treated – all have a life-long effect.

Organizations are social teams, comprised of relationships among people, even more so today with the growing percentage of service firms. Therefore, a leadership decision that may seem to affect just one person, will have a chain reaction and affect work teams, families, friends, and business associates.

Does this mean that leadership decisions must give priority to their effect on human resources? Not always, because decisions have to be made for financial, production, and competitive reasons for the sustained vitality of the firm. It is usually in the best interest of all of the resources, human as well as other resources, to preserve the economic health of the organization.

Alex Miller, a noted authority on business strategy, expresses this fundamental idea in his book, *Strategic Management*, with the succinct phrase, "No margin - no mission." If the organization is not generating material resources (margin to renew itself), there will be no sustainable organization (to carry out the mission that is important to the human resources). This idea works for both profit and not-for-profit organizations.

Have you continued to improve your leadership skills?

Review and update your leadership tool kit . . . the Old Angler's wisdom of sort your tackle box.

Two anglers are fighting their way against wind and waves.

Riding In The Passenger Seat

Perhaps you have seen the start of a competitive fishing tournament in person or on television. More than one hundred boats: Tracker, Lund, Crestliner, Triton, Ranger, Stratos, and many other brands form a long line according to their starting numbers. When the official starter gives the signal, they each, in turn, blast away at over fifty miles per hour.

What an awesome sight!

Drivers have it easier because they know where the boat is going; they can hang onto the steering wheel for support, and they have the experience of having done this before.

The passenger, however, is at the mercy of the driver. There is water splashing over the side and uncertainty because most passengers have been the drivers of their own boats. They are not prepared for sudden turns and there is very little to hang on to for support. Suddenly, the passengers feel very insecure; the drivers are in control.

The first time I rode as a passenger in a professional fishing tournament was an eye-opening experience.

I was not in control and felt very insecure. I was used to being in a leadership position and riding in the passenger seat made me examine my apprehensions and their relation to leadership. I did not like this new role.

Leaders are the boat pilots of their organizations. They have a better idea of where the organization is going and can make adjustments in route, can rely on the organization for resource support, and have usually had the experience of handling an organization in challenging conditions.

Followers are the passengers in the organization's journey. What it all comes down to is that they are at the mercy of the leader, the availability of resources, and the changing conditions. They do not have very much to support them because they have fewer organizational resources.

Sam Anderson, a professional angler, in one tournament asked me as we were charging along at 40 miles per hour in three-foot waves, "Doing OK? Do you want me to slow down a little?" What a welcome comment!

I suggested, "What if we slowed down just a little and attacked the waves from a better angle to get a smoother ride?" Sam did just that and we were in better physical condition when we reached the fishing area.

Leaders can make the ride so rough, both physically and psychologically, that the followers are not in shape to achieve results. Followers need to be heard; they have good ideas also.

One way of generating good ideas is to adopt a policy that future managers must first work at entry level positions to gain experience in understanding what customers really want. These positions may be in customer service, retail stores, or prospecting for new customers. Once these employees have "ridden in the passenger seat," they will have a much better awareness of customer needs.

A college student accepted a job in a combination mini-mart and gas station to pay college expenses and qualify for the company's college scholarships. The job also provided a learning opportunity for the student who planned a career in marketing after graduation. She made many observations and wrote them in her daily log of "lessons learned."

Her performance was so outstanding that the company's Director of Marketing offered her a product manager position in the company's headquarters after graduation. Where did she get most of the excellent ideas she suggested to the Director of Marketing? Her source was "lessons learned in the passenger seat."

Consider the followers . . . the Old Angler's wisdom learned from riding in the passenger seat.

A muskie lure, torn and battered after many days of fishing, is resting on a dock.

More Than A Pretty Face

Crankbaits spend their day being jerked around and chewed on. They are battered by rocks, gouged by toothy critters, and frequently jumbled together with other lures in dirty tackle boxes. The better they perform, the more they are exposed to hostile elements.

A muskie guide showed me a Suick muskie lure that was missing almost 90 percent of its walleye-like paint and looked more like a stick than a proven muskie lure. The owner prized it because even in its tattered condition, it was the most effective lure in the tackle box. Ripped and battered, it could still influence fish to strike.

However, battle scars will eventually affect performance. A deep gouge here, a cut there, a misalignment of the eyelet attached to the leader will change the lure's performance characteristics. It will not be as effective. You have to be alert to these changes.

Effective leaders are frequently stressed by the problems of running their organizations. They have hidden battle scars: health, anxiety, and relationship problems resulting from their leadership roles. It is not easy to face the challenges of dealing with people every day. Although leaders' battle scars are not on the surface, they are still there.

Let's take first-line supervisors. They are caught between the demands of upper management and the operational employees. They can't seem to win. When they please upper management, they get criticized from below; when they support operational employees, they get criticized from above. They are chewed on from both ends. The better they perform, the more they are thrown into tougher battles.

The old Peter Principle that people are promoted to their level of incompetency is not valid today. The demands of today's organizational environment require performance. People have to perform to be the kings and queens of the hill and they have to perform to stay there . . . and they have the battle scars from the competition.

Leaders have to be alert to their followers' real and potential battle scars. They have to be sensitive to stress problems such as job burnout before they become serious enough to jeopardize performance or even one's health.

Factors causing stress are more common today than ever before:

Employees such as those in the Bay Area of California may have to commute three or more hours each day through increasingly congested traffic because of the high cost of housing in metropolitan areas.

Mom and dad might both be working creating child care and other stress producing problems.

Basic changes in this technology driven economy are

causing even more rapid introduction, expansion, and decline of firms with resultant layoffs, job relocations, and underemployment.

These conditions cause battle scars; you need to be watchful.

Battle scars are signals of potential problems . . . the Old Angler's wisdom of more than a pretty face.

Rocks and vegetation provide hiding places for spotted bass waiting to pounce on unsuspecting baitfish.

Great Pitch

Tom Weise was teaching me how to fish for spotted bass (spots) in a California reservoir. We were using pink plastic worms that were Texas rigged, a particularly effective terminal tackle when fishing in heavy cover such as dense vegetation. Spotted bass like to wait in the shade, hidden by cover, and pounce on unsuspecting forage.

You want to get your tackle down quickly and in the right location so if there is a spotted bass lurking, hopefully it will strike. You also need to look for shaded areas. These are easy to find because the walls of most reservoirs are fairly steep, block the sun, and shade the banks particularly in the early morning and late afternoon.

We used a pitching technique to reach difficult areas such as the one shown in the illustration. We wanted to pitch the worm to a very small opening between two rocks and just short of the rushes. This technique involved holding the rod in one hand and the rig in the other and in a coordinated move, pitching (with an underhand throwing motion) the rig to the desired location. This is an effective technique up to about fifteen feet.

I had considerable difficulty learning this technique, but was making progress. After one particularly skillful pitch that resulted in a three-pound spotted bass, Tom said, "Great pitch." He knew a great pitch, and I knew he knew a great pitch. His comment meant a great deal to me.

    A respected leader is in a particularly favorable position to be a positive reinforcer. Think about the time that someone you respected told you that you made an important contribution. You knew in your own mind that you had done a good job and you knew your leader knew it.

    Your leader's comment more than reinforced your own feelings; it was magnified and created a lasting impression. There was a pleasant glow of satisfaction and a favorable, lasting impression bonded both of you.

    Have you had the same impact on others? No one knows if an opportunity to praise will come again.

    Praise has other dimensions. We have suggested that leaders do not know the effects their words of praise will have on another person. They may think the words will have little impact, but in reality, they may create a life-altering impact.

    A teacher wrote a note to a high school graduate using the phase, "You have an unlimited future!" The graduate took this note and placed it on the window frame of his dormitory room at college where he could see it every day. The student graduated with honors and wrote the teacher that this phrase had inspired him every day during the four years of college.

    Five simple words, but both knew that each word was a sincere expression of praise, caring, and concern. They were not just five simple words, but words that had special meaning.

Relationships also require a "great pitch." Ken Blanchard, co-author with Spencer Johnson of *The One Minute Manager*, one of the best-selling business books of all time, emphasizes positive reinforcement in all aspects of one's life, especially in relationships. "Catch people doing something right . . . and positively reinforce that behavior."

How have you made a "great pitch" in the last few days?

Do not waste opportunities to praise . . . the Old Angler's wisdom of the "Great Pitch."

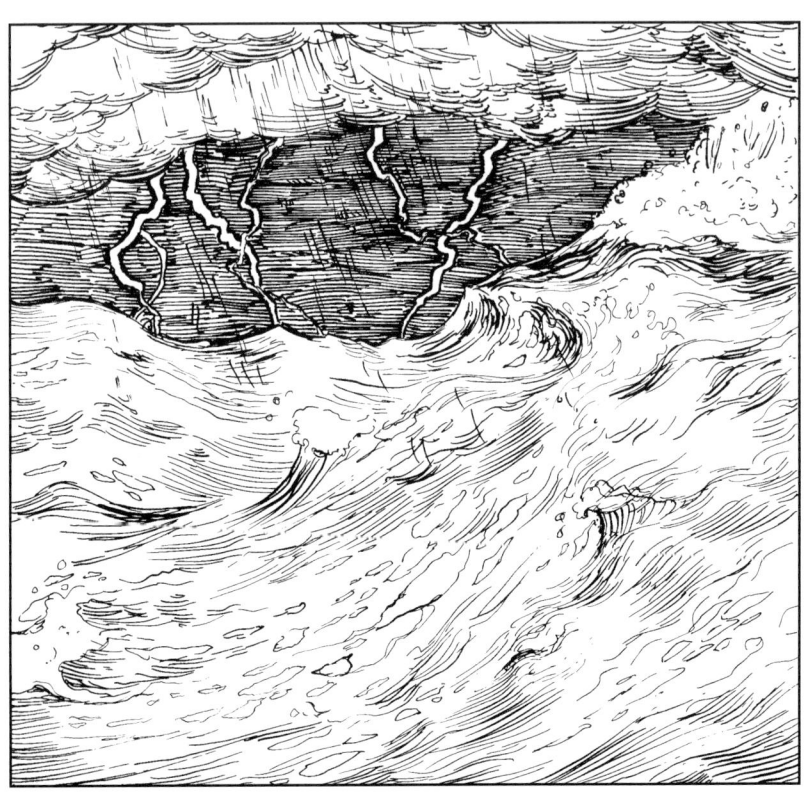
A fierce thunderstorm moves across a lake.

Thunder Drives Them Deep

A storm with thunder and lightning is an enemy of good catching; it drives fish deep and into difficult-to-reach locations. The accompanying waves stir up the sand making it unlikely for fish to see the lure. Vegetation is ripped away from weed beds; dirt and debris are washed from banks. Fish leave weed beds and go out into deeper water. The prospects of good catching are reduced.

Perry Smith, an outstanding muskie angler, and I were searching for trophy fish in early June. Our experience a few days earlier indicated that the fish were in sandy bays where the sun had raised the water temperature two to five degrees above other parts of the lake. However, there had been three days of fierce thunderstorms and the bays were brown with suspended sand and vegetation.

We searched in more than fifteen bays, but encountered the same unfavorable conditions. Thunder and lightning coupled with forty mile an hour winds had ravaged the fishing locations and driven the muskies into deep water. The fish that were accessible last week were very difficult to find. Thunder and lightning had driven them deep.

Bombastic leadership, like thunder and lightning, drives people deep, hiding within themselves to avoid possible danger. The swirling storm of threat and retribution clouds people's judgments and makes them less likely to voluntarily perform their tasks.

Avoidance behavior becomes the norm. If followers are unable to see what might possibly happen to them, they will be unwilling to act.

When people are hiding from the "thunder," increased sick leave, turnover, and absences may occur. Productivity is reduced. Just like weather patterns affect fishing, leadership can also affect performance. Leaders need to remember that members of their organization walk out the door every day.

If you do not meet your followers' expectations for career opportunities, challenging work, and fair compensation, other leaders will meet them.

It used to be that the only door open for most employees to return to was yours. They had no options. Employees today have far more choices. There are more open doors and incentives attracting them to new employment opportunities. They do not have to put up with the thunder and lightning.

Some employees are not affected by an organization's "weather." They will report to work rain or shine. Others need nurturing. They need a supportive environment in which to work.

There is a parallel in fishing. In the spring, certain parts of a lake warm faster than other parts, frequently by two to five degrees. If you go to an area of a lake near a sun-bathed sandy shore in a back bay, you can measure a temperature increase. The fish will be more active than in colder areas of the lake. The warmer water has nurtured fish just as a supportive work environment nurtures employees.

Many times it doesn't take much to show support for your followers: a thank you, a note saying "well done," a smile, remembering what is happening in their life can make a big difference in an employee's attitude.

Reduce the bombast . . . the Old Angler's wisdom of thunder drives them deep.

The wake trails behind as a fishing boat moves to another location.

Triggering A Response

Some anglers are avid hunters, searching all over a lake or stream looking for fish. After a few minutes if they don't get bites in one promising location, they go to another and yet another. By the end of the day, they are frustrated and tired. What they are trying to do is trigger a biting response. If they do not get this response quickly in one location, they go on to another.

Their backs ache from all of the pounding through the waves and their arms are sore from lifting and dropping trolling motors. When asked how the fishing was, they will dwell on all of their chasing around the lake with little or nothing to show for it. Chasing is not catching.

An angler's initial objective in trying to catch fish is to trigger a biting response. The angler wants both a strike and a hookup. There are many ways such a response can be triggered and the number of ways is increasing every year. Let us look at a few.

One way is movement that imitates life. A crawfish moves along the bottom in a certain pattern with claws forward with its tail slightly up. Wounded baitfish such as shad move in an erratic pattern.

This means that you should imitate life in your fishing. When the water is cold, you have to retrieve a lure slowly.

Certain fish like smallmouth bass react to a rapid retrieve, an oval-bodied crankbait, and a small lure. Largemouth bass seem to prefer a slow movement, more minnow-like shape of the crankbait, and a large size. Walleyes respond to small, slow moving baits and lures fished just off the bottom. Larger fish react to larger lures.

Newer techniques trigger fish to strike and become hooked These include salt-impregnated soft-plastic lures such as Berkley PowerBait. Examples include lizards, lures with life-like eyes such as the Real Image Livin' Eye System, and the Possum Panfish from Possum Lures that imitate baby panfish. New techniques are developed each year in the anglers' and manufacturers' quests to help initiate a triggering action.

We have defined leadership as the ability to influence individuals and teams to reach an objective. What is it that triggers influence for a leader?

It is power. Power is the "horsepower" of leadership because it elicits a triggering action for followers. Power may seem an inappropriate word because it may suggest brute force, but this is only one very small dimension of power.

Think of the power in the whispered phrase, "I love you!" It can be so soft that the listener can barely hear it. Lips close; there is a scent of emotion and perfume in the air, and perhaps even some gentle touching – a very powerful trigger! Think of finesse fishing for crappies – a very sensitive bobber, and almost invisible line, a very small lure, and an ultra-quiet approach.

Just as there are many different fishing techniques, there are many types of power. Personal power such as the ability to use data (expertise), access to data (information), and being liked by others (referent). There is also power that comes from the organization (legitimate), ability to provide items of value (reward), ability to provide access to others in the organization (connection), and ability to reprimand (coercive).

However, all of this power merely gives you potential to influence. Power is influence potential. Just because you chase around a lake looking for fish doesn't mean that you will catch any.

Just because you have the latest scent-impregnated soft-plastic worm does not mean that you are going to catch a largemouth bass. It is up to the bass. Just because you have world-class expertise in Web design doesn't mean that you are going to be hired.

Whether people are actually influenced is up to them. Power gives you the <u>potential</u> to influence in fishing and in leadership.

Power is only influence potential . . . the Old Angler's wisdom of triggering a response.

The favorite fishing spot that will be remembered again and again.

The Favorite Fishing Spot

One year, on the last day of vacation, three of us including my wife, Joan, and Terry Gill, a guide from Ontario Wilderness Houseboats, had phenomenal success fishing over a reef swept by a strong west wind. In just over three hours, we caught and released many walleyes. The reef just off a small island was a fishing paradise. Everything seemed to work: spinners, plugs, and spoons. It was one of the most wonderful days of fishing that we had ever experienced.

We dreamed of that fishing spot all winter and could hardly wait to fish it again the next summer. In fact, it was the first place that we fished, but with very little success. The wind direction was right and the granite reef certainly hadn't changed, but there just were not as many fish as the previous year.

We were filled with disappointment as the dream fishing spot faded in the distance and we began the search for other locations.

The experience was shared with friends who reminded me that over the several months since we had fished the location perhaps two or three hundred other anglers had, perhaps, fished the same area. After all, the location wasn't a secret and other anglers had experienced success. Our "special" spot wasn't that special and most of the fish that were easy to catch had been caught.

We began to realize that conditions change. Fish move, sometimes considerable distances. What might be excellent fish-holding structures at one time of the year are rather poor at other times. For example, walleyes leave the sandy bays as the water temperature increases and move to deep-water reefs.

Some anglers fish only one spot. These are the ones who go out and return saying, "They're not biting," when in reality the fish may be deeper or just a hundred yards away. Anglers need to adjust to varying patterns of the fish. There is no perfect "forever" fishing spot.

You are not the only one attempting leadership in your department, branch, or office. Other leaders, both within and without your organization, are attempting to influence your followers.

Perhaps you have experienced one or two of your most productive employees leaving to work for someone else. Things are not always going to be the same. Change is part of leadership.

You can't expect to have the same team, year after year. You have to recruit qualified replacements, develop them into a smoothly functioning team, and prepare for the day that they, because of what they learned from you, move on to greater responsibilities.

There is a comment attributed to Mark Twain, the famous humorist, "The only person who likes change is a baby with a wet diaper."

Dan Sweeny, a vice president of International Business Machines, elaborated on the need for change by urging, "A never changing business, one that is constant, stable, and predictable, is a competitor's delight. If you do not change, people will anticipate everything you do in the future and beat you to the punch. You must be a leader of change. If there is no need for change in your job, there is no need for your job."

Embrace change . . . the Old Angler's wisdom of the favorite fishing spot.

A cast has just been completed and the angler is retrieving the muskie lure.

The Lesson

How do you like to be taught?

My preference is positive reinforcement of my progress. When I am doing something right, I like to be praised. When I was new to muskie fishing, a guide who also became my friend, Terry Gill, showed me the best techniques and reinforced me when I made progress.

Terry started by selecting a medium-stiff 7' 6" rod with a heavy-duty casting reel. The preferred line for casting was a braided, fifty-pound test nylon line with very little stretch. He selected a black and red Mepps bucktail jerkbait and then demonstrated how the cast should be made. Grasp the rod with both hands, reel up the line so the leader's swivel is just short of your rod tip, and reach back being very careful that you are clear of any obstructions. Muskie lures have very, very mean hooks!

Pick your target and throw the lure, releasing your thumb as the lure is about to reach its highest point. You do not have to throw it very hard. As soon as the lure hits the water, start reeling fast enough so the lure is just below the surface. This is particularly important if you are fishing in slop – an area where is there is extensive vegetation. When the lure is close to the boat, make a couple of figure 8s as described earlier.

My first several attempts were pitiful. My throw allowed too much slack and the lure hit the water on the back swing, slowed up the throw, and the lure flew only twenty feet. The next time I allowed too little slack and the snap swivel caught in the tip at the end of the rod and jammed thus causing the lure to hit the boat on the forward cast. If I didn't reel fast enough on the retrieve, the lure would sink into the slop and catch weeds.

Was Terry discouraged? No! Instruction and encouragement accompanied every mistake as we worked on my technique step-by-step. After about an hour, almost every cast was capable of catching a fish; certainly not as effortless as an expert, but good enough to do the job.

This coaching technique has a direct parallel in developing leaders. You explain a task, let your student try it, and step-by-step guide the fledgling leader. As the student demonstrates skill, reduce the amount of instruction, and increase the amount of encouragement.

Be careful not to praise before accomplishment; this is confusing to the student because it doesn't focus the student's behavior on the specific activity. Your role is to guide behavior toward specific desired outcomes.

A fishing rod has guides to direct the line from the reel through the rod tip. If the guides are too small, they restrict the line's smooth movement. If they are too big, they promote line twisting and wind resistance. They have to "guide" just the right way to create maximum casting performance: greater sensitivity, smoother castability, reduced line damage, increased hooking power, reduced line twist, and reduced wind resistance.

Applying this to leadership, you have to "guide" to create maximum follower performance: enhancing skill in accomplishing the designated task, improving motivation, and increasing desire to learn.

This is called positive reinforcement of desired outcomes. You observe someone you are attempting to guide performing the desired behavior and you reinforce this behavior with a positive comment. This increases the probability that the desired behavior will be repeated.

It doesn't mean that the person will do it right all of the time; it does mean that the person will be more likely to do it correctly in the future. I still make mistakes when casting for muskies – but not as many.

Positive reinforcement is free! It doesn't cost anything to be a coach. It just requires a mindset that you believe people learn better when you encourage desired behavior. In terms of value, positive reinforcement is very worthwhile because it works best and costs less.

Praise people who are doing things right . . . the Old Angler's wisdom of the lesson.

An egret searching for food on an algae covered pond in midsummer.

The Walking Egret

I was driving to the launch ramp of a favorite lake and saw an egret walking very, very slowly across a pond. The sight was so stirring that I stopped the car to watch. The air was completely still and the morning fog was hanging just a few feet above the water. The egret was searching for food in a completely quiet pond that was covered with thick green algae. Egrets must be among the best at catching fish. They really must do it for a living.

The egret's track was a random walk because it did not know where the next bit of food might be. There were two or three footprints in one direction and then a sudden change to another direction. There was no discernable pattern.

Organizations take random walks, more now than ever before. Why? The world has changed. Many companies base their primary revenues on products and services developed within the past five years; the pace is increasing. If you haven't made significant changes in your organization within the past five years, your competitors will.

Your search will not be as easy as walking across a smooth, algae-coated pond. It will be more like going over an unseen waterfall in a fragile canoe.

Egrets have to explore for food wherever it can be found.

Organizations have to abandon the structured planning techniques that were effective in the past. They have to learn, as the egrets have, that nourishment can be found in many different directions.

———◆———

The path to organizational nourishment will not be the carefully planned route of the past . . . the Old Angler's wisdom of the walking egret.

Catching Success

Through Change

Minnesota's state bird, a loon, glides along in the calm of the early morning.

Making A Change

The sun has been up for an hour and life is stirring above and below the lake's surface. Nearby, a loon is gliding along the edge of a weed bed making just enough of a wake to set the rushes waving. A turtle is sunning itself on a rock and dragonflies are whirling in the sky overhead catching mosquitoes.

What a beautiful morning!

However, this tranquil scene is about to change as a fishing boat is headed toward this area.

When anglers cast their lures into lakes, ponds, or streams and troll their lures in lakes, ponds, or oceans, they change the natural environment. They make a difference in that location with their first cast. They may be removing a fish if they are skilled . . . and lucky.

They may also be ripping up weeds, sensitizing a fish to a particular kind of lure, or snagging a lure and tearing a sunken branch from the bottom. The fishing location will never be exactly the same because people have been there.

Leadership, like fishing, involves making a change. People change their leadership environment when they initiate leadership. The situation will be different after they implement leadership and it can never be the same. The situation may be better or it may be worse. The point is that it will be changed.

This suggests that we need to consider our leadership actions. Our leadership changes other people's lives, hopefully for the better. We don't dump our sewage into a lake where we are fishing. We shouldn't dump our sewage of anger, unethical behavior, or personal gain into our leadership environment.

When we accept or take on the role of a leader, we are also accepting the responsibilities and obligations that go along with it. The most basic leadership responsibility arises out of the instant change from "me" to "we"; just a change in one letter, but what a difference it makes.

This change could be called the "flip" side of life. When "m" is inverted, it becomes a "w" and visa versa. Your world has really changed completely upside down with the new responsibilities and obligations when you become a leader.

It is the same with fishing. Before we make that first cast or initiate a special fishing technique, we are consciously assuming the responsibilities and obligations that go along with being an angler. These responsibilities include following the fishing regulations, protecting others' safety, and respecting the environment. There is no escape from these roles, either in fishing or in leadership.

We are responsible for our actions because we made the conscious decision to accept these roles. We decide to go fishing, to attempt to lead another person, or to begin a friendship.

It is true that in some relationships there is considerable prompting from others, as many married folks would agree, but it takes at least two people to continue the relationship.

Fishing, leadership, and relationships mean accepting roles and the responsibilities and obligations that go with these roles ... the Old Angler's wisdom of making a change.

The dynamic movement of waves and current in a channel creates better fishing.

Reading The Turbulent Waters

There is a channel along the Aulneau Peninsula that separates two large areas of Canada's Lake of the Woods. Because the north-south Continental Divide is south of the channel, water flows north and then on to Lake Winnipeg and Hudson Bay. There are some years when the water level is low because of lack of rainfall. When this happens the channel is almost dry and water flows north through another outlet.

However, there are other years when there is an abundance of rainfall and the current surges through the channel as shown in the illustration. Waves and current rebound off the channel's banks. All of this creates just the right conditions to confuse baitfish thus giving the game fish an advantage. This is one of my favorite fishing spots. The key is that the turbulent conditions create better fishing conditions because they attract game fish eager to eat the disoriented baitfish.

When the water level is high, a good technique is to drift through the channel using some type of bottom bouncer, a piece of wire with a weight to maintain contact with the rocky bottom. The bottom bouncer has a spinner tied to it with a hook baited with a leech, minnow, or worm. This technique has caught walleyes, smallmouth bass, northern pike, and perch . . . and an occasional muskie!

Anglers must be able to visualize environmental conditions. As water levels rise and fall over the years, conditions off an island may be favorable or unfavorable for certain species of fish. Low water may promote more weed growth and the accumulation of sand; high water may limit weed growth and scour the rocks of sand.

Each condition attracts different fish; perhaps walleyes for a sandy bottom and smallmouth bass for a rocky bottom. The vision of what may be happening beneath the surface may attract an angler to a certain spot when conditions are right.

Leaders have to be able to visualize what is happening. Just as an angler must read wave, current, and rock conditions to visualize what is going on beneath the surface, so must a leader discern potential opportunities. This is strategic leadership. It means reading the many environmental factors that affect your organization.

It is relative easy to lead when everything is calm and peaceful. There are few challenges . . . but also very few opportunities. Turbulent conditions such as we are seeing now create opportunities. New technologies are replacing the old. World markets are changing, people have expanding wants, and all of this turmoil is creating situations for new ideas to succeed.

I have been fishing when the water surface was absolutely calm . . . just like glass. It was pleasant to be out on the lake, but it wasn't very good fishing. In fact, the few days that I have had difficulty catching enough fish for shore lunch were days that the water was unusually calm.

Walleye anglers like days when there is a "walleye chop," waves one to two feet high. If there is too much wind, it is difficult to hold your boat position over a hump, a raised part of the bottom.

There have been days that we have had to use two sea anchors, one at the bow and one at the stern, to help us control the boat's drift over a reef. We would pilot the boat about five hundred yards on the upwind side of the reef, throw out the two sea anchors, and then move in a controlled drift over the reef using our Global Positioning System (GPS) to locate the reef. After we had passed the reef, we would pull in the sea anchors and do it again. One day we did this for six hours.

Changing conditions mean constant assessment of the environment . . . the Old Angler's wisdom of reading the turbulent waters.

*Professionals and their amateur partners
stand during the day's opening ceremonies.*

The Past May Not Be The Future

Through the years my friends and family have caught and released hundreds of walleyes. A few have been kept for shore lunch and some for an occasional fish dinner with family and friends.

Because of these past successes, I was very confident when I fished as an amateur in an In-Fisherman Professional Walleye Trail tournament. The competition was held in Lake of the Woods in the Rainy River near Baudette, Minnesota. Amateurs were paired with different professional anglers over a three-day period.

I met my first professional at the rules meeting the evening before the competition and again the next morning at the departure point. During the boat ride out to the initial fishing location, the pro inquired if I had done much walleye fishing. I proudly recounted catching walleyes in a wide variety of conditions over the years.

The pro listened with mild interest and then responded, "How many can you catch today?"

Employees going into new jobs expect to succeed. It stands to reason that if they did not have the potential to succeed, they would not have been selected for advancement or even been hired. For example, perhaps a college graduate has an MBA, several years of work experience, and was president of a major student organization. Certainly, past education, training, and work experience have helped prepare the graduate to be a better performer, but all of this has been mere preparation.

The central issue for the graduate is performance, "What can you today?"

It has been my observation that people have difficulty excelling in a new, more demanding situation, because achievement has been so easy for them in the past. High school students who have excelled with relative ease go on to college, but the competition is more challenging.

College and university graduates who go on to further education have demonstrated their abilities to achieve without major effort, but now must face very demanding assignments. Excellence in the past masks the difficulties of the present and future.

We have all had this experience on fishing trips. There are days when both hands are very busy – one hand reeling in a fish and the other hand keeping fish from jumping in the boat. Just kidding! But we have all had days of excellent catching and we all have had days that nothing would work, as the initial bite, "Catching Success," described.

Just as in tournament fishing, sometimes the best do not succeed. No matter how hard you try, nothing seems to work. Don't quit. Learn from the experience. Fish in a different place; try another technique. If the new job doesn't work out, don't quit; try another company or another career.

Past performance doesn't insure future performance . . . the Old Angler's wisdom of the past may not be the future.

What is the weather going to be like tomorrow?

The Weather Channel

There has been a major change in anglers' behaviors. Instead of just looking at cloud patterns, checking the soreness in their arthritic joints, observing the actions of bugs, birds, and animals; they are watching The Weather Channel. Even in remote fishing camps, the demand for up-to-date weather information has prompted camp owners to put in satellite systems.

A week or two before the fishing trip, you check the long range forecast. Then, as the departure time nears, you focus on the seven-day outlook and the three-day travel planner. The night before you try to match your clothing and equipment to the expected conditions.

Just before you head for the lake or stream, what is the center of attention? Years ago it used to be the coffeepot and the tray of sweet rolls. No more. It is the TV as you attempt to glean every bit of information on wind, precipitation, and temperatures.

You probably have spent more time learning meteorology from The Weather Channel than you did on any subject in school. You also carry a weather radio and listen to it frequently, especially if there is a storm on the way.

But what happens when you return home? Do you continue watching The Weather Channel with the same attention? Where is your weather radio? It is probably under your rain gear. Of course you monitor the weather, but it is just not as important in your life as it was when you were going fishing.

A leader's primary focus is on directing and supporting followers, individually and in teams, to accomplish tasks. When tasks are as important as going fishing, they get considerable attention. You are really involved with everything associated with them.

You check for possible problems (rain and storms), increasing involvement by your boss (temperature and wind), and how long they will last (three- to seven-day forecasts). The closer you are to the planned completion date, the more you monitor the conditions.

What happens when the task is completed? Does it get the same attention? No. You move on to other things while checking on the previous task's progress. If you stay fully involved with past tasks, you will not be performing one of the most important roles of a leader–envisioning the future.

A leader's responsibilities include envisioning the future and turning this vision into completed tasks in a never-ending cycle.

Leadership is future oriented, not past oriented.

The line of thunderstorms that threatened to disrupt this morning's fishing has moved on and so must you if you want to catch success.

Focus on the future . . . the Old Angler's wisdom of The Weather Channel.

*Waves crashing on a rocky shore
create excellent fishing opportunities.*

Trolling The Windy Shore

One of my favorite fishing spots in northern Minnesota is on Lake Kabetogama. This lake is part of the Voyageur National Park and the Wilderness Canoe Trail from Lake Superior across to the Minnesota-Canadian border, down Rainy River, across Lake of the Woods, and up to Winnipeg and beyond to Hudson Bay. This route was used by fur trappers and explorers.

One area of Lake Kabetogama has a long, sloping shelf going down about twenty-five feet from a rocky island. The shore consists mainly of broken granite or riprock. The prevailing west wind smashes against this shore and seems to confuse baitfish and sends them into shallower water, particularly along the reef. This stimulates the walleyes to feed and creates a very productive fishing spot.

Personal favorite techniques are trolling with both shallow- and deep-running plugs. Spinners with hammered gold blades using hooks baited with minnows or night crawlers also work. However, trolling is very difficult when it is windy because you have to follow the underwater contours of the reef, fight the wind and waves, maintain a desirable speed, and properly position the lure.

An effective trolling pattern is "S" shaped going over a depth from six feet to twenty-five feet in a way that moves the lure back and forth across the reef in a crack-the-whip pattern. You cannot take the chance of running aground and smashing your boat and equipment. Therefore, you steer your boat toward the reef and swing your lure in toward the shallower water and then out again along the reef before you repeat the pattern.

This trolling technique has another advantage. As you start a turn, your lure moves more slowly and sinks. When you complete the turn, the lure speeds up and rises. This enables you to cover different depths and to present your lure at different speeds.

There is danger in this technique, particularly if the wind is blowing above fifteen miles per hour and you are fishing alone. Your tackle is going to be snagged on the rocks and you have to be very skillful in retrieving it. The slightest miscalculation of position, engine problems, or gust of wind and your boat will be slammed against the rocks. If this happens, your boat will be hammered against the riprock again and again as each wave crashes into it.

If this happens, you must get out of your boat, stand on very slippery rocks, try to bring the bow around so it is pointed away from the island, push it far enough out so you can climb over the side, grab your paddle, and force the boat out into deeper water. Then and only then, can you use your motor to move into deeper water.

You will be wet and exhausted . . . but that's all part of the fun of fishing.

Just as fishing is often best in a changing, turbulent environment, leadership is also many times more productive in a changing, turbulent environment because there are many more opportunities. New technologies are introduced, new markets are open for development, and peoples' desires are stimulated for new products and services. It is a "happening" time.

When everything in an organization is calm and certain, people think, "Why change?" There is no stimulation, no motivation to change. Activities are going along on a predictable path to a predictable goal. It is business as usual. However, when things are not going as well, perhaps it is when business is declining, new competitors are challenging, funding becomes uncertain, that people start to rethink the status quo.

Unfortunately, as one friend told me, "People cling to the status quo long after the quo has lost its status!"

How can you initiate change in your organization? Ed Shein, a professor emeritus at the Sloan School of Management, Massachusetts Institute of Technology, Boston, described two anxieties people have regarding change.

The first is an unwillingness to abandon the present.

The second is an unwillingness to adopt something new.

Let's look at the first anxiety. Ed suggests that business as usual must be seen as the road to failure. If organizations continue to do the same old thing, they will fail. Therefore, the first step is to get people to realize the prospect of failure and be open to something better.

This "something better" must be so attractive and beneficial than the present that it overcomes the second anxiety, that of trying something new. This is where a credible vision comes in. People need to accept this believable future before they will leave the present. The two steps must work together: the present must be abandoned and the future must be embraced.

The leader must be careful. There is danger in this change process just as there is danger in getting too close to the rocks. The leader can make the fear of continuing business as usual so great that people become wary of doing anything new. People become locked into fear of any change no matter how beneficial it may be. They stay fixed on the present, something secure, something they know and trust.

In fishing, there is a way of reducing this danger. You can put down the bow-mounted trolling motor to act as a shield and troll carefully, not getting too close to the shore. Then, as you gain a better understanding of the underwater structure, you can move closer and closer to the reef.

The same concept applies to leadership. Test the water first without creating undue anxiety and as you better understand people's feelings and apprehensions, you can move closer into introducing new opportunities.

Introduce change carefully . . . the Old Angler's wisdom of trolling the windy shore.

Catching Success

Through Relationships

Two friends are building a lasting relationship.

Fishing Is For Relationships

How many times do you see a solitary angler? You may see this person fly-fishing by a stream because occasionally it is fun to be all alone to enjoy the quiet and peace. Most of the time, however, you want to be with friends.

Fishing is all about relationships. The fun of planning fishing trips as a family. The fun of getting a team of friends together, wearing crazy t-shirts, buying funny hats. The fun of giving presents such as a mailbox in the shape of a bass, a "gone fishin'" door hanger, and fish motif glasses and coasters. The fun of sitting around the ice fishing house telling stories. The fun of the evenings by the campfire.

When and where did your fun fishing relationships start? Many friendships go back for years. The illustration of the two friends fishing may suggest one of your first fun times. Perhaps they have ridden out to a small inlet leading into a lake, thrown down their bikes, placed their simple tackle box besides them, and started casting. What fun!

This might be the start of a friendship that will last them the rest of their lives. This may be the start of a love and a respect for fishing that will be passed down to their children and grandchildren.

I remember the first time my wife and I went fishing with our granddaughters. We decided to go to nearby Lake

Millerton to fish for spotted bass. The girls were apprehensive about handling the bait, but my wife and I made it a fun experience by first going to a bait shop where they could help us select worms, freshwater crawfish, and minnows.

Our fishing technique was to use a simple worm hook, light line, and a red and white bobber. After baiting their hooks with worms, I moved along rocky banks in about ten feet of water using the electric tolling motor while the girls let their lines trail behind the boat. The girls watched their bobbers very intently.

Suddenly, one of the bobbers plunged beneath the surface and moved diagonally away from the boat. We missed that fish, but one of the girls was successful in catching a sixteen-inch spotted bass within half an hour.

The girls were soon brave enough to bait their own hooks with worms, crawfish, and minnows. Crawfish were a special delight to the girls as we explained how they moved in the water and how the pinchers really wouldn't hurt their fingers.

In just three hours, the girls changed from not being too sure about fishing to, "When can we go again?"

Perhaps you have heard the expression, "Let work be like play." This suggests that work should have many of the same elements as play: joy of achievement, companionship, attaining goals, playing by the rules, and respect for others.

Leadership should also be like play with many of the same elements: ethical conduct, enjoyment of working with others, pride in developing followers' knowledge and skills, and mutual enjoyment of achievement. You do not lead alone. Leaders must have followers. You need each other.

———◆———

Fishing and leadership both depend on the rules of play . . . the Old Angler's wisdom of fishing is for relationships.

A fire pit is ready for the preparation of a shore lunch.

Shore Lunch Values

Shore lunches are one of the most enjoyable aspects of fishing. Bernie Freeburg, Dave Anderson, and several of my other friends like to spend the morning catching one or two eating-size walleyes for each person. We then look for a windswept point to build a fire, prepare a shore lunch, and relax. Fish that are not needed for shore lunch or for an evening meal go back into the lake.

Let them grow!

When it is lunchtime, we look for a place where it is safe to tie up the boat to protect it from damage. We build a rock fire pit like the one in the illustration, collect some wood, and start a cooking fire. After the fish are filleted, the potatoes and onions are peeled and chopped and the fire is banked to provide constant cooking heat.

We like to deep fry potatoes and onions together in a large cast iron skillet. While these are cooking, the fillets are dipped first in water, then, in turn, are rolled in flour, submerged in egg, and rolled in crushed corn flakes. The cans of corn and beans are opened and placed near the fire.

When the potatoes and onions are cooked, more oil and a little bacon grease are poured into the pan. When the right temperature is reached, the fillets are then placed into the skillet for a few minutes of cooking. The fish are done when the pieces are golden brown on both sides, normally about one minute a side.

What a meal! Golden brown fish, steaming potatoes and onions, hot corn and beans, bread with fresh blueberry jam . . . what a life!

When we are finished, we carefully extinguish our fire, and throw the fish remains and the uneaten food on the rocks where gulls and pelicans fight over them. Nothing is wasted; everything goes back to nature except the loose paper and other trash that we gather to take with us. The area is left just as we found it. We make one last thorough inspection just to make sure the fire is completely out, all cooking equipment has been packed up, and all waste removed.

We value our opportunities to fish together, share experiences around the cooking pit, and have a meal on an unspoiled island. We want to preserve this site for others.

The same principle applies to leadership. If you value what you are doing and believe what you and your organization are doing is important, don't you want to leave a legacy for the future? Don't you want future leaders who can make important contributions to the next generation?

It all comes down to one simple idea. Are your beliefs and values important? If they are, then you should plan for the future. If you do not consider your beliefs and values to be important, why bother?

We wanted to leave the shore lunch spot for future shore

lunches just as previous anglers had left this spot for us. This was one of our basic shore lunch values.

Lead for legacy . . . the Old Angler's wisdom of shore lunch values.

What fun to watch sunfish nibble on a worm in clear water!

Watching Them Bite

As a teenager, I was a counselor at a summer camp. The camp was located on the shore of a pristine lake where the water was so clear that the bottom was visible at least fifteen feet down. One of the side benefits of working at this camp was the opportunity to fish for sunfish early in the morning and in between sessions of the camp.

Fishing was very simple. One of the other counselors would join me at sunrise and we would untie a twelve-foot wooden boat, grab a pair of oars, and row about a quarter mile along the shore where there was a series of sandy points going out from extensive weed beds.

We would row very slowly and quietly, letting the boat drift along. Redwing blackbirds would be perched on the cattails warning the neighborhood of our approach. When we reached a likely location, we lowered the cement filled bucket we used as an anchor and began to fish. We didn't use any fancy and expensive gear. Our rig consisted of a simple cane pole, a black braided line, and a can of worms.

We would watch the fish nibble at the worm and, at the right moment, set the hook and add another fish for the lucky campers' dinner. We would also maneuver the worm to increase our chances of catching larger sunfish.

At times, it was a little difficult to see the fish in the early dawn because the sun's reflection off the water was quite dazzling. However, a friend provided a pair of polarized glasses that filtered this reflection and made it possible to see the fish as they hid in and around cover. We could see when it was necessary to add a little more line to reach close to the bottom or when to raise the pole tip to move the worm closer to a school of sunfish near the surface.

We were able to adjust our fishing techniques because we could see what was working and what was not.

Feedback is the polarized glass of leadership. Feedback helps you filter out what you think is happening from what is actually happening. There are many activities going on in an organization, some very important and many relatively unimportant. It is just like the much-preferred larger sunfish; you need to see and focus your energy on the projects that really count.

It is just not enough to identify high priority projects, you must also identify what it will take to get them accomplished. This means distinguishing what forces will help and what forces will hinder each project's implementation. Further, it means assessing the intensity or power of each helping and hindering force. It does little good to decide on a specific course of action and determine important helping and opposing forces to this course of action, without assessing how much the helping forces will contribute and how much the hindering forces will hold you back.

For example, your firm is introducing a new technology. Your executive team agrees with you that this is necessary to stay competitive. You also identify that using the technology will require extensive training (hindering force). Your first-line supervisors are familiar with the technology and support it (helping force). But what is the relative intensity of the two forces? Are your first-line supervisors so supportive of the new technology that they are willing to cope with the scheduling and other problems associated with extensive training, or is their support only modest?

You need feedback to make these determinations: what are the projects' relative priorities, what are the issues affecting their implementation, what are the helping and hindering forces, and what is the relative intensity of these forces?

You also need to see what is happening during the implementation process.

Are people responding to your leadership? Are your team's energies directed toward what is worthwhile? Are you getting the message that you may be off track? You need to be constantly assessing the true impact of your leadership through feedback.

Feedback helps tell you what is happening . . . the leadership wisdom of watching them bite.

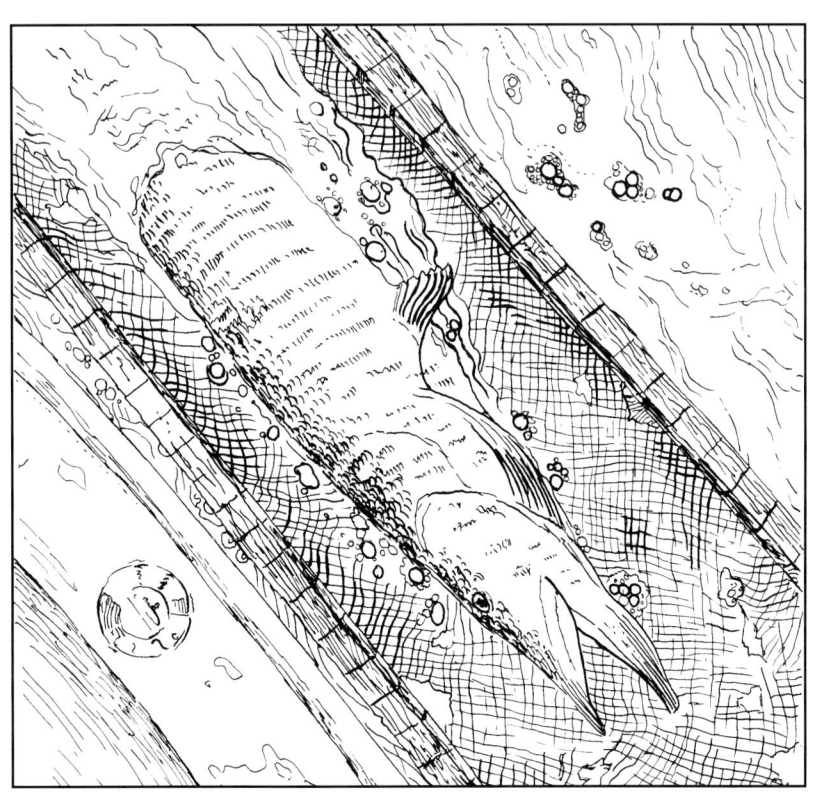

A powerful muskie in a cradle is about to be released unharmed.

You Get What You Give

My friend, Jerry Dotson, and I were sitting in a houseboat rented from Ontario Wilderness Houseboats in Morson, Ontario, Canada, waiting for the driving rain and blustery wind to subside so we could go fishing. The weather forecast indicated that the front would pass in about five to six hours.

We decided to pass the time by taking our fishing boat to Nestor Falls, about an hour's trip, and have lunch at Helliar's Resort. This would give us something to do and would be a new experience for Jerry. Besides, there was Helliar's Trading Post where we could look around at the many attractive gifts, especially the ceramic birds.

While we were having lunch in a very cozy, wood-paneled room overlooking Sabaskong Bay and watching the rain continuing to fall, the storeowner joined us and shared some of his fishing experiences during the last fifty-some years. He pointed out a beautifully mounted muskie hanging on a wall. His father had caught it in the late 1940s. He observed that today, in the early 21st Century, muskie and smallmouth bass fishing had never been better.

He told of conversations with his father and grandfather who had been some of the first settlers in the area. At that time more than half of the muskies were killed by rough handling when they were caught or kept as trophies. In the past ten or so years, he related, the kill rate was very low. This, he explain, was because limits were low, size regulations in Lake of the Woods did not allow the angler to keep any fish under 48 inches in length, guides urged catch and release, and superior handling techniques such as using a cradle helped keep the muskies alive.

Almost all of today's anglers have a conservationist attitude. They want to improve fishing success. They have supported specific conservation steps for smallmouth bass, walleyes, and other species. Fishing is excellent. For example, conservation licenses for a limited catch are now available, an extended closed season for smallmouth bass has been implemented, Catch and Release signs are seen along roadways, and there are size and number restrictions for walleyes.

The current emphasis on measuring a fish's dimensions together with catch and release protects the fish because you can determine its weight by using formulas such as those published by the Billings, Montana, *Gazette*. For example,

Walleye: length (times) length (times) length divided by 2,700
Northern Pike: length (times) length (times) length divided by 3,500

A 36-inch great northern pike would weigh approximately 13 pounds.

Weighing a fish requires much more handling than measuring it. This is why most anglers carry rulers or, as in my boat, have a ruler pasted on the rear deck. Anglers are realizing better fishing because they are willing to behave in ways that promote better fishing. Anglers are getting what they are giving through their own behaviors. Responsible angling behavior will lead to better catching; irresponsible angling behavior will lead to reduced catching.

There is a new program related to catch and release: CPR standing for Catch, Photo, and Release. If you want to resuscitate declining fish stocks, practice CPR.

You as an employee get what you give in your work. If you would like to have greater freedom to perform your job with little supervision, then you have to behave in a responsible manner. If your behavior is characterized by missed work assignments, poor quality, and indifferent attendance, you will attract close supervision. You determine the type of leadership you will receive.

You determine your fishing and leadership experiences . . . the Old Angler's wisdom of you get what you give.

A mature bald eagle surveys his domain and protects his nest.

Let The Eagles Fly

It was one of those mid-summer days when everything seemed perfect. It was a day when it was great to be alive and to be fishing: no phone, no interruptions, no need to look at a clock - a time just to enjoy! Don Erickson and I were fishing for bass around a small, rocky, and wooded island. In the sky a mature bald eagle soared in the updraft and then swiftly perched on a dead pine tree.

While we continued fishing and following the curve of the island, we saw a nest off in the distance. It was difficult to tell, but wasn't there an eaglet in the nest? What an impressive scene!

Fishing was put out of mind as we continued observing the eagles while the boat drifted with the wind toward the southeast. Just off to the right there was a sheltered, sandy cove. Our first reaction was that this would be a perfect spot for camping or mooring our houseboat. Upon reflection, however, why disturb the family of eagles? Disturbing the eagles now might endanger their habitat for our grandchildren and others to enjoy.

Upon further reflection, we would have been wrong to move our houseboat into the sandy shore. It would have meant sacrificing the long-term joy of observing the eagles many times over the years and sharing the experience with family and friends. If we had succumbed to thinking only of ourselves, of acting expediently, of being self-centered, many wonderful opportunities would have been lost.

Self-centered expediency is really a poor reason to lead. Short-term advantage may result in short-term gain, but seldom provides for sustained eagle watching. Leaders must avoid the short-term perspective. They must think not only of themselves, but also of others, particularly the followers.

One name for this attitude is servant leadership. The idea is that the leader is the servant of the follower, not the other way around. This changes the whole focus of the leader's role from command and control to development. When one focuses on leader rather than leadership, it means focusing on self rather than on others.

Perhaps you know of leaders whose desire for accomplishment lets nothing stand in the way of success. They are impervious to all suggestions. They are invincible in their drive for implementation at all costs. Their employees talk about their trampling staff, lacking integrity, and grabbing credit from others.

- In their minds, they could do no wrong.
- They made every decision.
- They made themselves the center of the company.
- They believed the end justifies the means.
- Truly, they were bosses from hell.

There is a world of difference between a strong ego, which is essential, and a large ego, which can be destructive. Leaders with strong egos know their own strengths.

They are confident. They have realistic ideas of what they can accomplish, and they move purposefully toward their goals.

Leaders with large egos are always looking for recognition. They constantly need to be patted on the back. They think they are a cut above everybody else; they talk down to the people who work for them.

What could these leaders with large egos have done differently? They could have been more open to feedback so they wouldn't place so much emphasis on mastery, looking good, and trying too hard.

Perhaps they should have insisted on a board of directors with qualified and involved outsiders who would have kept them focused. Perhaps they should have hired more executives willing to challenge them. Perhaps they should have listened to people who reminded them that they were the servants of the organization, not the masters.

Leadership means influencing others, not oneself. Winning the hearts and minds of others means placing your primary attention on them, not on you. True servant leadership means that leadership is a you word, not an I word.

Servant leaders would not have disturbed the eagles' nest for self-gain.

Practice servant leadership . . . the Old Angler's wisdom of let the eagles fly.

The different rock and vegetation around an island attract different species of fish.

Every Island Has Opportunities

Perry Smith, a very experienced muskie angler, fishes for muskies when the season opens in May until the late fall, totaling more than 150 days a year. Perry enjoys fishing in Sabaskong Bay, Lake of the Woods, near Morson, Ontario, Canada.

One day when we were searching for possible muskie habitat, Perry reminded me that every island has a habitat for holding worthwhile fish. It might be a small area of rocks and rushes not larger than a living room or it could be an expansive sand bay. The habitat might not be suitable for a huge muskie, but it might be for a smallmouth bass.

Perry commented that people have the same characteristics as islands. Some people may have developed many favorable attributes, while others have very few. The skilled leader's task is not only to identify worthwhile attributes, but also to bring forth the best that people have to offer. The person's contribution may not be an innovative strategy that will change the entire direction of the organization, but it may be a useful contribution.

It is the accumulation of these small, but important, suggestions that supplies the continuous improvement required by organizations. The leader's role is to bring out and recognize the best in each person. This enables each individual to be a meaningful part of the entire team.

There is much more emphasis on diversity today, not in the context of reducing prejudice, but in the context of the rich variety of ideas, skills, techniques, and opportunities that diversity brings. How many of us eat the same breakfast cereal every morning? How many of us have the same food for dinner every evening? We want variety. We are nourished by it.

One city in California has over one hundred different ethnic groups speaking more than forty different languages. What a wonderfully rich environment in which to live and grow!

Have you wondered why Perry, who fishes almost exclusively for muskies, was so attuned to the habitat for other fish species? Despite his reputation, Perry is not just a muskie man. I have learned through my many fishing trips with Perry that he is unusually sensitive to the ways of other fish species, the wonders of nature, and the joys of the outdoors. He doesn't charge around a lake. He pilots his boat carefully and deliberately to get the most from each day's experience.

Perry's careful assessment has a parallel in leadership and relationships: be mindful of snap judgements. Participants in my leadership seminars frequently ask what I have learned from years of college and university education . . . and they want me to state it in one sentence. My response usually is, "I have learned to wait ten seconds before saying or doing something stupid!"

Initially, this may seem like a small benefit from higher education, but upon reflection and discussion, it really is a powerful lesson. Education, travel, awareness, experience all contribute to a broader picture of life and a realization that things are usually not what they first appear to be.

How many times have we been too hasty to criticize, too quick to put forth one's own opinions, too eager to tune out another's contributions. If we had waited ten seconds, perhaps our leadership efforts would have been successful or a relationship would have been continued.

Ten seconds; so little to gain so much.

Don't ignore people's potential; diversity is organizational nourishment . . . the Old Angler's wisdom of every island has opportunities.

Duck Bay Lodge on Hay Island in Sabaskong Bay, Lake Of The Woods, offers an outstanding vacation experience.

Happy To Catch Just One

Liz, our oldest daughter, had never fished with me in the northern Minnesota and southern Canadian areas. She had, however, heard dozens of stories about many fishing trips over the years and had seen countless pictures of trophy fish, fantastic scenery, and had heard about the expertly prepared and very delicious shore lunches. I was finally able to arranged a fishing trip at a time when our two busy schedules would permit.

Perhaps her expectations would be too high; I was very concerned when she arrived to spend a week fishing with me. What might she consider as "successful fishing?" This was in my mind as we crossed the lake late in the evening to Duck Bay Lodge. There wasn't time to share my apprehension with her that evening as we prepared our cabin.

As we started across the lake on our first day of fishing, I asked Liz what she would like to catch. "Oh, I would be happy if I caught just one," she responded. We went to a gap between two islands and started trolling spinners for walleyes. After about an hour, Liz caught two fish for shore lunch and a twenty-three inch walleye that we released.

It was the largest walleye of the trip.

She was delighted and I was very proud. She was already far beyond her expectations. We had a two-hour shore lunch and then spent the rest of the afternoon cruising around the lake.

The next afternoon we trolled for northern pike using crankbaits. I drove the boat and maneuvered it so we would run parallel to a series of shallow weed beds that dropped off rather sharply into deep water. Call it "beginner's luck" or what you will, but Liz hooked a big fish and despite getting her line tangled, brought a thirty-three inch great northern pike to the boat. We took pictures and released the monster.

It was the largest northern of the trip.

It was raining the next day, but Liz wasn't concerned as she commented. "I have my rain gear, so let's go fishing." We caught several smallmouth bass that day. Who caught the largest bass? Liz. When we talked about her success, she was delighted, but repeated, "I looked forward to quality time with you, Dad. I would have been happy to catch just one."

What are your followers' expectations? Are they higher or lower than yours or those of the organization? It is important that leaders and followers understand and communicate their levels of expected performance. Too high an expectation will mean that it will never be reached. This will result in frustration for both leaders and followers. Too low a level will mean that important goals will not be achieved. This is why it is important to talk things over and to reach a meeting of the minds.

This does not mean always matching your expectations.

The lesson I have learned fishing with Liz is to letting go of my goal for her and to appreciate Liz's triumph in accomplishing hers. There is peace and celebration in letting go, at times, of your ideas for success and accepting another's feeling of accomplishment. Sometimes it is better to accept their success and not impose your standards.

Leaders also want to know if their expectations are realistic or not. This suggests that leaders should assess and diagnose their situations in a manner similar to physicians. Prescription without diagnosis is medical malpractice. Leadership without assessment and diagnosis is leadership malpractice. The readiness assessment technique introduced earlier in "Matching The Hatch" is a vital part of successful leadership.

All of my concerns regarding Liz having a great fishing trip should have disappeared when I heard her very simple, direct expectation. What joy we experienced together as she reached beyond her expectations!

Leaders should also experience mutual joy when employees reach and exceed expectations.

Assess expectations . . . the Old Angler's wisdom of happy to catch just one.

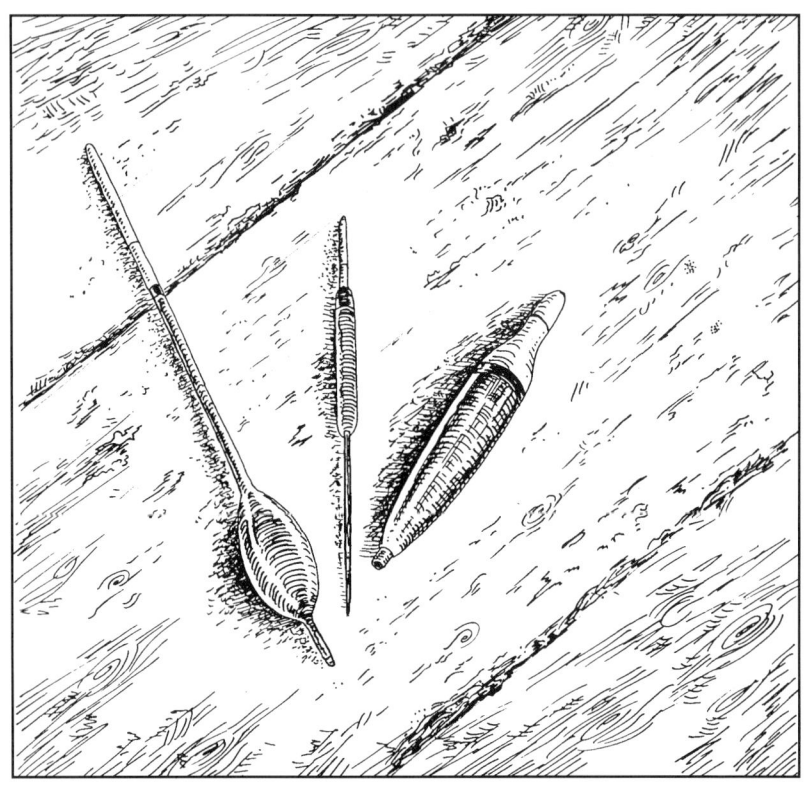

Thill balsa wood bobbers are available in many sizes and shapes.

Sensitizing Your Bobber

Have you ever seen a videotape or television program demonstrating the Thill Gold Medal balsa floats available from Lindy-Little Joe, Inc? These floats were developed for use in fishing competitions, especially in Europe, where it is important that fish should not feel even the slightest opposing force when they nibble on the bait.

Thill floats are very sensitive and indicate very small movements, a highly desirable characteristic when fishing for panfish, particularly bull sunfish. The floats are usually made of balsa wood and have a very distinctive shape as shown in the illustration on the facing page.

A type of fishing that is growing in popularity is attempting to catch fish that weigh twenty to one hundred times the breaking strength of the fishing line. Fish weighing over two hundred pounds have been landed using four pound or lighter line.

This technique requires very sensitive playing of the fish with the drag or tension of the reel set below the line's breaking strength. The slightest jerk on the line will cause it to break. This is sensitive fishing at its extreme.

What kind of bobber do you use when you are leading? Is it a traditional big red and white one that takes a major pull to indicate a nibbling or biting fish? Or do you use a

Thill that is highly sensitive and will react to a very small movement?

How attuned are you to what is happening around you? Being in tune with followers is a very important leadership behavior as shown in the following example.

A mid-level executive in a high-tech Internet company was on the fast track, but had the potential to move up even faster. The executive was told by the chief operating officer of the company that she didn't know enough about the people in the organization. The executive wondered about this and the difficulty of knowing more about the several hundred people in her Division, but she decided it was worth a try.

The executive studied five personnel files each day. At the end of a month, the executive knew about the background of more than a third of the employees.

Now the executive could say, "Paul, we appreciate your contributions during the ten years that you have been with our company." "Mary, congratulations on your recent promotion." Magic happened. Employees became more willing to share feedback. Performance and productivity increased. The Division became a team.

Did this work?

She is now the chief executive officer of a major U.S. company and her personal stock holdings are worth more than $20 million.

This same approach can be applied to relationships. Have you gone fishing with your family members, preferably one at a time? "Happy To Catch Just One" describing my fishing experiences with my daughter, Liz, illustrates this important point. Our relationship is much stronger because we have spent several weeks fishing together. And, by the way, you will learn more about yourself through these relationships.

Increase your awareness . . . the Old Angler's wisdom of sensitizing your bobber.

Sandwiches, chips, cola, and fruit are the back-up for lunch if the fish are not biting.

Better Bring A Sandwich

Minnesota's Mille Lacs Lake is one of the most outstanding walleye fishing lakes in the United States. Sometimes, however, even the very best lakes have periods when the fish are not biting.

An example of this was a feature story in the July 5, 1998, Minneapolis *Star-Tribune* sports section reporting that Mille Lacs anglers harvested (fish kept versus caught and released) .11 pounds per angler for an hour of effort during one forty-five day period.

This meant keeping a one pound walleye for every nine hours of fishing. Because a good shore lunch requires about two pounds of walleye per person, there must have been many anglers who went hungry. Hopefully, they brought a sandwich or two!

These statistics were probably a surprise to most readers who expected that one would easily catch lunch on one of the very best lakes for catching walleyes. However, the same article reported that in 1992, one of the better years for fishing, more than half of the fishing trips on Mille Lacs resulted in no walleyes.

What must the statistics be in an average or poor lake? Anglers better bring a cooler filled with sandwiches!

A valid expectation anglers have when they go fishing is that they will catch fish.

A parallel can also be found in leadership. When people attempt leadership, they expect they will get results. However, as we noted earlier, just as anglers may return empty-handed, people may not be able to influence others.

Dave Ulrich, Jack Zenger, and Norm Smallwood in their book, *Results-Based Leadership*, cite Peter Drucker's comment, "Leadership is all about results." They suggest that:

Effective Leadership (equals) Attributes (times) Results

They note that leaders must demonstrate attributes and achieve results. Leadership attributes include factors such as skills, competencies, and values that have a clear parallel in fishing.

What results do you expect? It is an established leadership fundamental that results should be achievable, perhaps with a little stretching. In other words, results should be meaningful targets.

If you expect to catch a legal-size muskie every time you go fishing, you will be very disappointed. Expert muskie anglers suggested that one might reasonably expect to catch a muskie in about every 1,000 casts. Catching a trophy muskie normally requires 10,000 casts and many anglers have fished all summer without catching any, let alone one that met the minimum legal standard.

Of course, you might get lucky and hook a trophy

muskie on your first fishing trip, but the odds are against you.

Effective leaders understand what can reasonably be expected. They set targets that are difficult, but attainable, and they concentrate on developing people's attributes to achieve these results.

Match expectations to achievable results . . . the Old Angler's wisdom of better bring a sandwich.

A marlin reaches for the sky off the Great Barrier Reef in Northern Australia.

A Day Meant To Be Shared

The day was the culmination of years of dreaming about going marlin fishing off the Great Barrier Reef in Australia. It had taken almost two years for me to save enough money to hire a boat and crew. Normally, when one goes deep sea fishing on a charter, fishing access is shared with the other anglers on the boat.

You draw straws or decide on some method of who handles the pole on the first strike or you rotate poles every hour. This way, everyone gets an equal chance at fish hitting the outriggers or the shorter lines just behind the boat. There are many different schemes and the charter captain usually suggests a fair procedure.

But on this day I was the only client and with only the Captain and one deckhand, set off on a forty nautical mile trip to a likely fishing area. There were only a few cumulus clouds, the wind was less than fifteen knots, and the waves were only about three feet with a modest swell. The conditions were almost perfect.

The first strike came about noon. We could see a marlin chasing the left outrigger's lure. It was close enough so we could see the lure's stream of bubbles and there was strike after strike, but no hookup. This was repeated several times during the early afternoon. Several strikes, but no hookups.

Then, about 3:00, we had success. A marlin slashed at the lure a couple of times, grabbed it, and we were able to set the hook.

I do not want to tell a fish story; it wasn't a world record approaching fifteen hundred pounds, but the captain estimated the marlin at about two hundred and fifty pounds.

I fought the marlin for over an hour before bringing it close enough so the captain could cut the leader. I was relieved as I slumped down on a hatch with shaking arms, aching back, and hands that could hardly turn the reel handle. But as I reached for a cold drink, I experienced a sudden wave of sadness.

This was a day that really needed to be shared with people who cared.

The many fishing companions who should have been there to share the joy, laugh at my physical weakness, join me in a few cold ones, and remember the day that would be refreshed in memory were not along. It was a day of special emotions as the boat motored up the Cairns estuary, marlin flag flying, and carrying the thrill of a once-in-a lifetime experience.

Marlin fishing has its parallel in leadership. There are special thrills when a major sale is landed, when a new product is launched, and when a long-planned-for acquisition is completed. Just as in marlin fishing, you don't do it alone. You have to have experienced executive leadership and a firm that can provide the resources for you to have the opportunity for a success.

Share the experience. Thank those who have contributed. Teach less experienced employees how it was done in a way that they could share the excitement. Major achievements are normally few, but they can be the vision for others.

Spread the joy of special achievement . . . the Old Angler's wisdom of a day meant to be shared.

All of the tools and parts are laid out on a towel so nothing gets lost as we get ready to change propellers.

When Trouble Strikes

During a hearty breakfast of pancakes, sausages and hot coffee served by a roaring fire, my friends and I talked about fishing plans for the day and decided to fish some twenty miles up the lake.

It took about thirty minutes after breakfast to get all of the gear stowed, life jackets on, bait on board, and everyone settled in the boat. The wind was blowing about fifteen miles an hour with some white caps on the open water. The weather forecast was for clearing conditions.

We were cutting through the waves at about twenty-five miles per hour and had just rounded an island to turn northeast on a new course when to everyone's dismay, there was a bump and a loud crash. The stern drive kicked up and the boat rocked from side to side. We had hit something.

At first we thought it was a submerged log or "deadhead," but as we checked for hull leaks, we found that the boat had hit a chimney, a three-foot diameter spire of rock that rose almost to the surface. It was not on any chart. We had passed over this same area many times in previous years, but the water level was lower this year.

There we were, dead in the water, as helpless as a turtle on its back. We were two miles from the nearest shore in water sixty feet deep and the wind was increasing in velocity as a squall line started moving across the lake. It began to rain with increasing intensity. We put up the canvas top and side curtains, lowered the 24-volt electric trolling motor, and with the help of the waves and the motor made it to a sandy beach.

When we inspected the outdrive, we saw that the propeller was badly damaged. One of the blades had been partially sheared off, and five inches had been knocked off the skeg, the lower part of the motor housing that protects the propeller. While the rest of the party huddled under cover, I stripped down to my underwear, climbed over the side into the chilly water, installed a spare prop, and checked for damage by running the engine at a very slow speed.

Fortunately, I was aided in this repair effort by loud cheers and help with selecting and handing tools, and shouts of "Our hero!" We had survived a major problem by being prepared and knowing what to do. "We trusted you," said one of the anglers.

Trust is an intrinsic part of influencing because people must be able to trust you, believe in you, and depend upon you before they respond to you.

Let's take the power of rewards for example.

What were the rewards the fishing party gave me while I was repairing the damage? Encouragement, praise, help with tools, a cup of hot coffee, dry clothes, and many shouts of "Our hero!" They could have remained huddled under the canvas cover complaining about the misfortune, but they realized that they were literally "all in the same boat." They turned what could have been a very disagreeable situation into a mutual adventure and we left the cove in great spirits. Their attitudes enhanced our relationships.

Did I mention that the sun came out a couple of hours later?

People trust you to be fair and impartial in distributing rewards. This issue of fairness is critical because people know what should be fair; they know what is going on in your organization. They know what is right and what isn't right. Therefore, leaders must exhibit all of the elements of fairness: consistency, openness, and even-handedness. Leaders must be careful not to raise even the slightest suspicion of unfairness.

Whether one is fishing or leading, the journey to success is seldom smooth. There are hidden dangers and changes in environmental conditions happening as water levels rise and fall, economic conditions ebb and flow, and trends come and go. Leaders must promote confidence in their followers so that they can handle both day-to-day issues such as fairness or challenging, unexpected problems.

Trust goes with the territory when you are a leader.

Develop trust by being prepared . . . the Old Angler's wisdom of when trouble strikes.

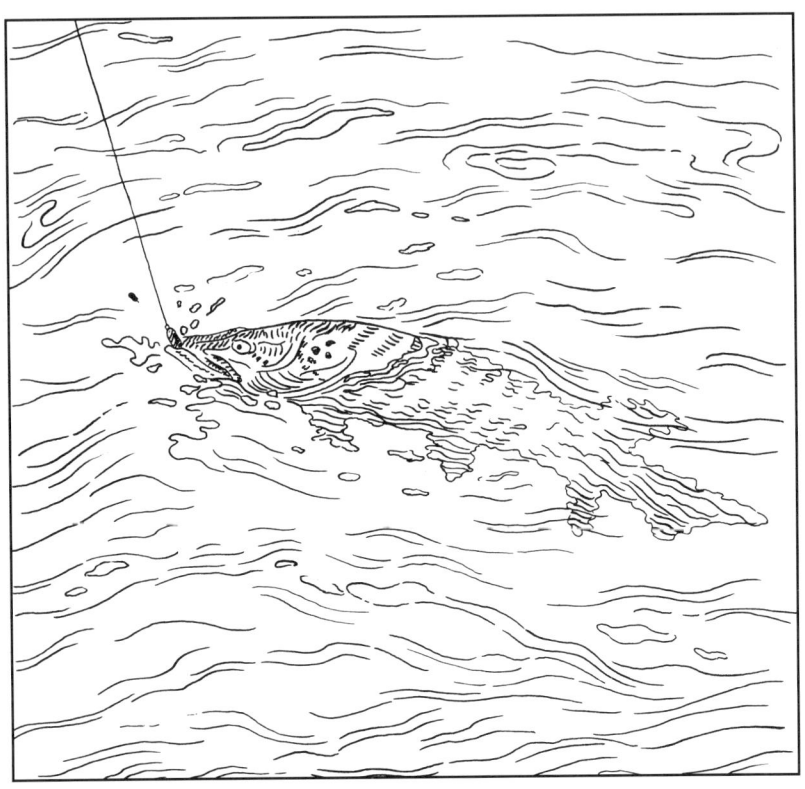

Muskie are solitary fish that become more difficult to catch as they get older.

Targeting The Generations

Experienced anglers know that it is much easier to catch young fish that have been recently stocked into a stream or lake than it is to catch more mature, experienced fish. Young, hatchery-raised fish will bite on almost anything they perceive as food. For example, rainbow trout are fed white corn in the hatchery and when they are released, they will bite on a small, number 8 hook baited with white corn.

Older, larger fish are a much different challenge. Usually, they are more solitary. They tend to inhabit different lake locations than smaller fish, they are more aware of motor noise and move away from it, they prefer a larger lure, and they are more selective in what triggers them to strike. They did not get older, larger, and wiser by attacking every object that was dragged near them.

Usually is an important word. It is important because there are no hard and fast rules in fishing. Some young fish are difficult to catch because otherwise they would not develop into larger fish. Some older fish are easy to catch because it is the spawning season and they will strike at anything that comes near. These exceptions break the so-called "rules."

Leaders today face the daunting challenge of leading the generations, each with special motivation needs. Because of these special motivational needs, there are no hard and fast rules. Ron Zemke, Claire Raines, and Bob Filipczak in *Generations at Work: Managing the Clash of Veterans, Boomers, Xers, and Nexters in Your Workplace*, have contributed to these guidelines.

Generation G : Ages 54 and older. The Gray Generation. These are the people near or beyond retirement age. They love to work and they have very significant contributions to make. Many need to work to supplement a modest pension income. They are concerned, however, about being led by younger leaders. After being in authority positions most of their lives, it is difficult for them to be in a follower role. Younger leaders need to understand these concerns and lead with compassion, respect, and awareness.

Generation B: Ages 35-53. The "Baby Boomer" generation. Some have already taken early retirement. Others find themselves with less retirement income than they had expected. Security is a critical issue with mergers, downsizing, pension plan changes, care of elderly parents, and many other challenging issues.

"Where do I stand?" is an often-asked question by Generation B members. Leaders need to take time to discuss this issue. Frequently, they are the same issues that most leaders themselves are facing.

Generation X: Ages 23-34. These beneficiaries of technology want to be self-led. They want to know where the organization is and where it is going. They want to make a contribution. This is why it is important that organizational leaders communicate and share their vision.

Micromanaging will not work. Generation X'ers will walk because there are just too many opportunities available. They want to feel the entrepreneurial spirit of being a vital part of the organization.

Generation Y: Ages 12-22. The "Yes Generation." They might also be called the "S Generation" because they comprise so many of the service providers. Teens and early twenties want to work to pay for cars, music, clothing, and the other perceived necessities of life. They feel they are competent and they are. Generation Y should be evaluated on demonstrated performance and moved along quickly to being self-led. They want to feel responsible and most are very responsible.

The special needs of these different generations suggest that there is no one best approach to leadership. Each generation has different characteristics; a one-size-fits-all approach just doesn't work. Leaders must tailor their leadership approaches to the followers. A size 48 long suit will fit some, but not very many. A directive approach will fit some, but not many.

Leaders have to be flexible to adapt their styles or approaches as the situation requires.

Focus for successful leadership . . . the Old Angler's wisdom of targeting the generations.

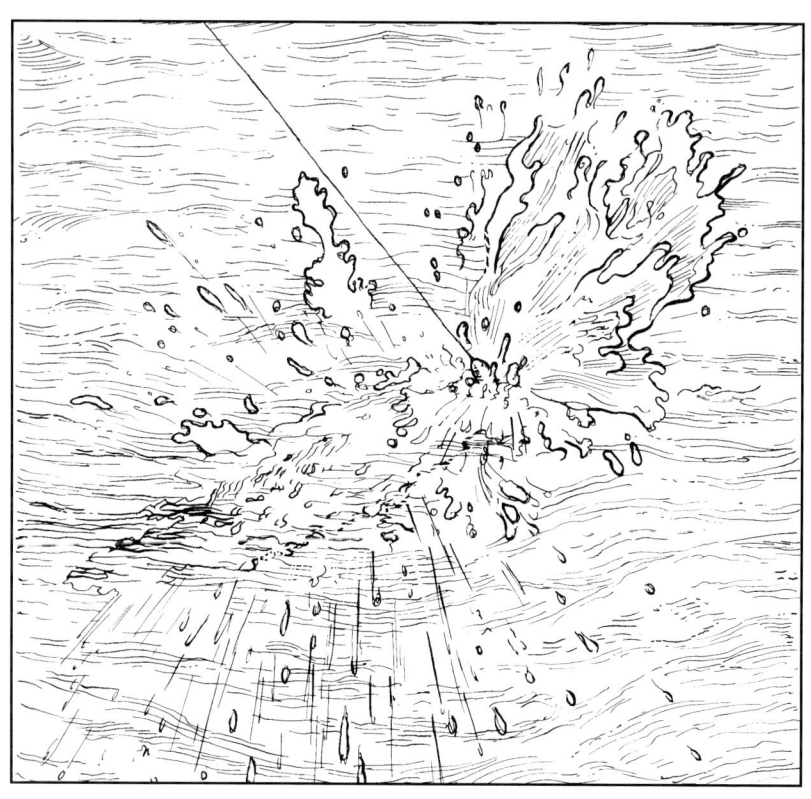

*The fish was on just a second ago!
But, with a huge splash it was gone!*

Overcoming Disappointment

I remember how I used to go fishing in a twelve-foot wooden boat on a small lake during my growing-up years in western Minnesota. Bullheads and perch were my usual catch although occasionally I caught a largemouth bass or small northern pike. One day when I was eleven or twelve years old, one of Dad's friends asked me to go fishing. I was very excited to be going. This was going to be a fun experience!

We used the old wooden boat and a seven and one-half horsepower outboard engine. There was not much action as we trolled along weed beds using spinner rigs with silver Junebug spinners and minnows. We were both getting discouraged when a great northern pike hit my rig and after about ten minutes, I had it by the side of the boat. However, in netting the fish, my Dad's friend unintentionally knocked the pike off the hook. My fish, the largest one I had ever had on my line, swam slowly away.

"Why did you do that! It would have been my biggest fish. You should have been more careful!" I sulked and pouted for the rest of the afternoon. It was the last, and only, time Dad's friend asked me to go fishing.

Many years later I was fishing in a northern Minnesota river with my father-in-law, Frank Watson. It was early March and the ice was beginning to go out. In just a few days the season was going to close for a month. There were large ice floes in the river and it was very, very cold. Both of us were bundled up in the warmest clothing we could find. We were wearing heavy mittens, arctic parkas, and cold weather boots. Fishing was good and we caught and released several two to four pound walleyes.

"I've got a snag," I yelled. "It's moving!"

After a fierce battle, the largest walleye either of us had ever seen was brought to the boat. "Get the net!" There was no net. "Grab the gill covers!" My father-in-law reached for the gill covers with his mitten-covered hands, missed, reached again, knocked the walleye off the hook, fell halfway into the river, and had to be lifted by his belt back into the boat. There were no words to be said as we returned wet, cold, and disappointed back to the dock and home.

Recalling this experience reminded me of the first time I went fishing with my future wife. I was so eager that even before the boat was stopped, I had my line in the water. My "honey" was trying to get organized when I called out for her to help turn the boat around because of a snag. As the boat turned, I realized that it was not a snag, but a huge walleye.

"Get the net!"

The net was filled with clothing, lunch, and fishing gear. Five minutes later, the net was cleared. I called out, "Remember, fish do not swim backwards. Net the walleye head first!" I put the walleye in perfect position to be netted, but my inexperienced fiancé slashed at the fish, knocked it off the hook, and it was lost. We were both devastated.

However, a wedding did take place and our next anniversary will be our fiftieth. We still laugh about the first time we fished together.

Several years later we were fishing with my Mom and Dad. We were trolling for walleyes and northern pike. It was a beautiful, lazy mid-summer day and we were trolling in and out of the shadows cast by tall pine trees close to rocky islands. My parents were using spinners with hammered gold Indiana blades baited with fat head mud minnows, my wife was trolling a Rapala crankbait, while I was using a spinner with a large, two-inch pearl blade.

As we worked our way around a rocky point and headed toward a weed-filled bay, there was a tremendous strike. A very large fish, either a northern pike or a muskie was on the line. At first, we thought it was a muskie. It took about half an hour to bring the fish parallel to the boat.

It was a northern, the absolutely largest one that any of us had ever seen! There were four of us fishing in an old-style fourteen-foot wooden boat. There was not enough room for this over thirty-five inch fish and us. Reluctantly, we played the fish for almost forty minutes until it broke the line. We were disappointed, but not angry. The fish probably would have capsized our small boat. Our safety and our belief in catch and release came first.

Each of these "bites" illustrates the importance of relationships. There cannot be so much emphasis on getting the job done that interpersonal relationships are destroyed.

At the same time, there cannot be so much emphasis on relationships that the objective loses focus.

The first "bite" illustrates this point. The opportunity to fish again with my Dad's friend was lost because I put so much emphasis on landing the northern. Angry words and unwarranted comments destroyed the relationship with Dad's friend. In the second and third experiences described above, I had matured and while there were disappointments, they did not destroy relationships.

In the last "bite," fishing was placed into perspective so while the objective was important, safety in the boat, and a greater objective of sustaining the species were accomplished.

Care must be taken to sustain relationships . . . the Old Angler's wisdom of overcoming disappointment.

Catching Success

Through Reflections

This illustration shows one of the many signs that promote the increasing awareness of "catch-and-release" fishing.

How Many Did You Catch?

What do people ask you when you return from a fishing trip? "How many did you catch?" "Did you limit out?" These questions focus on quantity of catch rather than quality of the catch or of the experience.

If your purpose is to have enough fish for a couple of meals when you return home, great! You have a justifiable purpose. But if your purpose is to catch as many fish as you can to "one up" someone else, then you are tainting the majesty of fishing which includes basking in the sunshine, feeling a cool breeze coming over the water, and enjoying the glow of a setting sun.

How many activities bring with them the great outdoors, the satisfying healthy meals, the companionship of friends, and the thrill of feeling the strike, playing the fish, bringing it to the boat, releasing it to catch another day?

The American Sportfishing Association (ASA) reported that the two major reasons people go fishing are for relaxation (35 percent) and for being with family and friends (33 percent). Fishing is really the basis for developing relationships.

A wonderful quality about fishing, unlike many outdoor sports, is that it doesn't cost very much to get started. Fishing is within the financial reach of everyone. You can enjoy all the glory of fishing with just a simple cane pole, fishing line, hook, bobber and bait. Or, you can spend thousands of dollars on boat, motor, and equipment and enjoy competitive fishing.

You do not have to catch fish to enjoy the fishing trip. My wife and I like to fish in the California Delta, a wonderful area with many species of fish just East of San Francisco next to San Francisco Bay. One day we were fishing for striped bass using ghost and other types of shrimp. The air temperature was about sixty-five degrees and the sun was shining with very few clouds. We anchored in the current, folded out our seats, and decided to take a brief nap.

An hour later we woke, checked our baits, and our hooks were bare. We both had strikes while we were sleeping! Was the trip a failure because we didn't catch any striped bass that day? Absolutely not because we had fun being together . . . the real purpose of the day.

Leadership is also a majestic activity. What satisfaction being the leader can bring when you realize that someone or an organization believes enough in you to respond to your leadership efforts! You can enjoy being a leader in a simple outdoor setting or in a corner office on the 60th floor in mid-town Manhattan.

You have followers. How fortunate you are!

Some individuals are so ego-centered that they believe they can "limit out" by satisfying their own egos through self-centered activities. They always want to get their way, are careless about their behavior, trample over rules and regulations, and show a general disregard for others.

There is a difference between being confident and being egotistic. Leaders need to be confident in their own actions. Very simply, if you are not confident in what you believe, why should others be confident?

Egotism is another matter. An egotistical person leads for self-purposes. Perhaps you have observed that many persons are egotistical because they lack confidence. They are insecure and they take it out on others. They are the ones, perhaps, who emphasize quantity in terms of "limiting out" rather than in the quality of the fish or the joy of the fishing experience.

Consider the purpose of "limiting out" . . . the Old Angler's wisdom of how many did you catch?

It is time to park the boat and take a short rest after an exciting morning of fishing.

All Others Are Bait

One of my favorite fishing experiences in the summer is to troll for smallmouth bass off small islands. This is not the usual approach because most bass anglers like to cast, spin, flip, or use some other technique. However, trolling offers a relaxing way of enjoying the outdoors. You can observe nature and it is an effective way of catching bass when trolling crankbaits such as the Rapala Shad Rap.

One August day when the lake was relatively calm, I headed for a series of small islands that appeared to hold some promise for good fishing. Parts of the shorelines of these islands were exposed to the prevailing northwest wind. On most days, it was too rough to reach this area and the waves were too choppy to fish it effectively. I decided to troll along the islands rocky shorelines using a Rapala #5 Shad Rap, the deep running perch model.

It was still quite windy with about two-to three-foot waves making it difficult to control the boat. My trolling plate mounted over the propeller slowed the engine, but increased the control problems.

The fishing technique was to troll in a series of loops around the island, sometimes close to weed beds, sometimes over points. Five bass were caught and released in about an hour. Each time a bass was caught, I had to increase power and move away from the island so that the boat would drift past and not crash on the rocks. When I was clear of the island, I would reduce the power, retrieve, and release the bass.

I was kept very busy!

A sixth bass was hooked and the same routine was followed. But this was different. There was a much greater pull. Perhaps the bass was trailing heavy weeds? But this didn't act like a bass. The pull was much heavier and the line began to shake. Was this a northern pike "shaker head?" The fish was brought to about ten feet from the boat. There was a flash of yellow. Was this a huge walleye? No, as the fish approached the boat, I saw a northern pike of at least fifteen pounds, but where was the bass?

Two feet away from the boat, the northern spit out a three pound smallmouth bass, circled the bass a couple of times, while the bass, still hooked, dashed about excitedly. The northern then swam away. I released the bass and reflected about the "once in a lifetime experience." It probably was a "once in a lifetime experience" for the bass also!

To the northern, the smallmouth was just bait. To a smallmouth, small perch are just bait. To a muskie, walleyes, perch, and small northern are just bait. Should leaders "fish" for bait (intermediate goals) or should they try to achieve end results? The Old Angler suggests end results and there is a parallel in fishing.

Bait is an intermediate step. Frequently, perch and walleyes occupy the same general area. If you want to catch perch, place your bait above the bottom where they are suspended. If you want to catch walleyes, get down to just above the bottom. Catching perch when you are after walleyes is a distraction. Concentrating too much of your resources (bait and time) will hinder you from your goal of catching walleyes.

In an organizational context, too much concentration on secondary and less important goals will use up your organization's resources and hinder you from reaching your primary goals. Here is another example.

I was fishing with a guide for barramundi in a river near the Australian City of Cairns, near the Great Barrier Reef. The first step was to capture bait. We used a throw net, a small mesh net with a diameter of about eight feet weighted with small pieces of steel around the edge. Using an oar, we poled the boat very slowly and quietly toward areas where we could see the baitfish moving. Then, we threw our nets over a school of baitfish and hauled in up to a dozen.

When we had enough bait, we went after barramundi. In this example, baitfish were essential to catching game fish, but they were not the main objective. While it was fun to catch baitfish, the reason we were on the river was to catch barramundi.

———◆◆◆———

Don't be overly distracted by secondary objectives . . . the Old Angler's wisdom of all others are bait.

Rod, tackle box, fishing vest, and hat are on the dock waiting to be put away for another season.

Being The One

Another fishing season has come to an end. It is time to close the tackle box, clean and put away the rods, winterize the engine, and store the boat. Will there be another season? Who knows what the next year will bring?

This is a poignant time when you can reflect upon the past months in the outdoors. As the seasons pass, more time is being spent enjoying the totality of nature. As a result, each year seems to bring better fishing because we are more attuned to the habitat, the movement of the currents, and the seasonal patterns of fish. Each season seems to bring an increasing respect for the beauty and peace of nature, and increasing communion with its majestic environmental forces. Each year finds that more is given back as the fishing experience is shared with friends.

This has been a book about relationships. Relationships with nature, friends, and family.

How empty is the telling if there is no one to tell?

How barren the boat if there is no one with whom to share it.

How superficial the experience of a shore lunch if one is eating alone. Relationships are much richer when they complement each other.

Thoughts are with the many people who had the foresight to establish rules and regulations improving habitat, fishing access, and emphasis on catch and release. There have been many contributions that make fishing the enjoyable experience it is today. To repeat a previous theme, we all are beneficiaries of the servant leaders of the past who gave back far more than they gained.

Have you reflected on your leadership legacy? Have you thought about the contributions of the many courageous men and women who have contributed to your wellbeing. These giving men and women saw the need for action, believed in what they were doing, inspired others and, in spite of many difficulties, made your organization, your community, and your country better than it was before.

This is the essence of leadership. These forward-thinking men and women sought leadership roles and accepted the responsibilities that were vital parts of these roles. They understood the leaders' duties – to take the values they believed in and made meaningful change happen.

The song, "Be the One," written by an unknown author, can be adapted to express the essence of leadership: to be the one who gives back, to be the one who develops meaningful relationships, to be the one who accepts the challenge.

In a world full of many problems
where solutions are hard to find;

For every challenge that is met,
there are many left behind.

And though it seems that no one cares,
it still matters that you do;

Because there is a difference you can make,
the choice is up to you.

Will you be the one to answer the call?

And will you lead when those around you fall?

Will you be the one to make your team succeed?

Tell the Old Angler . . . will you be the one?

Answer the call of the leadership challenge . . . the Old Angler's final leadership and fishing wisdom . . . be the one.

Afterthoughts

This has been a book about developing the knowledge, skills, and attitudes to improve your "catching success" in your fishing and leadership. It has also been a book about relationships and about developing the trust that binds you to people who care about you and whom you care about in return.

We all have moments when we say or think, "I wish I could do that over."

I have had those thoughts when, upon reflection, I wish I had spent time fishing with more of my friends.

I have also had those thoughts when reflecting on my leadership experiences. Perhaps I should have spent less time in my office and more time walking around the plant, listening to concerns and sharing ideas.

I have also had these thoughts when reflecting on my past relationships. What could I have done to put more attention on others rather than myself?

The illustrations and text in *Catching Success* have been prepared to give you opportunities to reflect on your fishing, leadership, and relationship experiences. It is my hope for you, my reader, who has shared this time with me, that these illustrations and words have helped you recall special relationships, revisit memorable fishing trips, and remember important leadership contributions on your lifelong journey to *Catching Success*.

Glossary

Angler: A person who fishes with a pole or a rod and reel.

Baitfish: Any fish that is normally eaten by a larger game fish. Examples include different types of food fish such as shad.

Beads: Round glass, plastic, or metal objects threaded on a line to attract fish through color and/or sound. For example, beads used on a Carolina rig slide up and down a line between a sinker and a swivel to create noise that attracts fish.

Blade: An oval shaped spinner made of different materials, usually metal, attached to the arm of a spinner bait that provides both flash and vibration to attract fish. It can be smooth or dimpled (hammered).

Bobber: A plastic or wood device that is attached to a line to keep a rig a certain distance from the bottom. The bobber floats on top of the water and moves (bobs) when a fish strikes.

Bottom Bouncer: A device made of a metal wire, a weight, and a swivel for attaching line that is used to keep bait or a lure close to the bottom. The tip of the device is used to "feel" and bounce along the bottom.

Carolina Rig: A soft bait, usually plastic or a worm, rigged on a 16 to 36 inch leader below a barrel swivel, plastic/glass bead(s), and a heavy slip sinker.

Cast: A technique that throws or moves a line and its lure to a desired location.

Catch and Release: The environmentally sound practice of removing a fish from a hook and placing it carefully back into the water to live and fight another day. Also known as CPR: Catch, Photograph, Release.

Cover: Weeds, lily pads, and submerged branches, for example, that provide shelter for fish.

Cradle: A device used to protect a fish as the hook is removed prior to its release.

Crankbait: A lure that has a bill on the front that allows it to dive when it is retrieved (cranked using a reel) to prompt fish to strike.

Crawfish: A small freshwater crustacean.

Fishing pressure: The ratio of anglers to fish in a given area of a body of water. The higher the number of skilled anglers, the more the fish are pressured which usually results in a limited catch.

Flip: A casting technique where the lure (normally a pig and jig or worm) is thrown underhanded (flipped) to place the lure in a difficult to reach spot.

Floats: Another name for the general class of bobbers.

Fly fishing: A fishing technique that uses lures made of different materials such as feathers, thread, and animal hide to resemble the food on which game fish feed.

Forage: Live food that game fish eat, i.e. crawfish, minnows, and insects.

Game fish: The fish that are sought by anglers for the sport of catching them, i. e. largemouth bass, rainbow trout, northern pike.

Guide: 1) experts hired based on their knowledge of the body of water and fishing expertise; 2) circular attachments to a fishing rod that direct the line from the reel to the rod tip.

Hit: A fish striking a lure.

Ice auger: A tool used to cut a hole in the ice.

Ice fishing: Fishing through a hole cut in the ice. Modern ice fishing is usually done in ice houses that may range from simple to very elaborate.

Jerkbait: Lure that creates erratic, diving motions when retrieved (jerked).

Jigs: Small metal-headed lures that are bounced along the bottom or fished in an up and down motion. Bait, i.e. worm, shrimp, minnow, is usually attached to the jig.

Launch ramp: A (usually) concrete "driveway" that extends into the water and is used to maneuver a boat off and on to a boat trailer.

Leader: A section of line that is usually smaller in diameter and lighter in breaking strength than the main fishing line and is attached by a swivel. The purpose of a leader is to create distance between a sinker, bead(s), or swivel and the hook or lure.

Leader board: A board that displays the standings of a fishing tournament.

Limit: The legally declared number of fish of different species that an angler is allowed to remove from a body of water. Limits differ on different species of fish and local, state, or national laws.

Limit out: To reach the number of fish one is allowed to take. For example, in one state the limit on salmon is "two in possession." Once an angler catches and keeps two salmon, the angler must fish for another species of fish.

Line: The material used to attach a rig to a rod or reel. The line may be as simple as a piece of string attached to a stick or a monofilament/braided line.

Line strength. Also known as test strength or tensile strength. It is the static breaking strength of a line. Anglers fishing with low test lines have caught amazingly heavy fish because they set the drag or brake on their reels so the line would be allowed to go out before it would break. Anglers select their line based on the game fish species they are seeking.

Live well: A holding tank on a boat that takes in water and usually includes an aeration system to keep fish alive.

Lure: Any artificial bait used to attract fish. Live bait is frequently used in combination with a lure.

Matching the hatch: Making the lure similar in appearance to the food that game fish usually eat.

Outrigger: A device used to hold a line away from a boat to increase the area covered during trolling and/or to separate fishing lines.

Pig and jig: A jig with a plastic skirt and a piece of colored pork/plastic to promote strikes.

Plastics: Lures made from plastic designed to resemble worms, grubs, crawfish and other possible forage.

Playing a fish: Bringing a fish to the angler in a manner that keeps the line from breaking and the fish on the line.

Plugs: Lures made of wood, plastic or other material. Usually equipped with one or more treble hooks.

Presentation: The art of positioning the bait or lure in a manner that is most attractive to the fish depending on the species, season, water conditions, depth, and structure.

Rig: A general term for a wide range of terminal tackle such as a Texas rig. Can also be the boat itself.

Reel: A device attached to a rod that is used to spool line. Includes a mechanism (crank and gears) that allows line to be released or retrieved.

Retrieve: The act of taking in line usually with a reel mounted on a rod.

Riprock: Also known as riprap. A term given to piles of rock or other material that are placed near shorelines or breakwaters to prevent erosion. It is also a term used to describe broken rock along a shoreline.

Rod: A length of wood, plastic, bamboo, or other material that is used to hold a reel and to make it easier to cast a lure further and more accurately. Rods vary in their action (flexibility).

Season: The legally defined time period when a species of fish is made available for catching. There are limited seasons for some game fish and open seasons for others.

Shad: A baitfish that is a stable food of bass and other fish.

Sinker: A weight attached to a line or a lure to promote its fall toward the bottom of the body of water.

Slop: Heavy aquatic vegetation.

Spawn: A period of time when fish reproduce. Spawning usually involves building a nest and defending it (also known as a spawning bed).

Spinner: A lure or rig that spins while being retrieved to add noise, flash, or vibration to attract fish.

Splitshot: A weight split almost in half for easy attachment and removal from a line.

Spoon: A metal lure that attracts fish through flash and vibration when it is retrieved.

Structure: The physical features of a body of water. The term, for example, includes humps (mounds rising from the bottom), rock piles, and points (underwater extensions of land).

Swivel: A small metal device tied to the end of a line that allows for movement of a lure or for the attachment of leaders.

Tackle: A general term for the lures, hooks, weights, and other devices used to catch fish. Excludes the rod and reel.

Texas rig: A type of rig generally used to fish plastics where, for example, a hook (s) is buried in a plastic worm to avoid snagging weeds and tied to a leader with a weight positioned two or three feet up the line.

Tie a fly: Making a fly using parts of feathers, fur, thread, and other materials to imitate the natural food of fish. The fly is tied to a tapered leader.

Top water lure: A lure that is designed to be retrieved on top of the water to create noise, flash, splashing which attracts fish.

Troll: Dragging a lure/rig behind a boat using a line. The weight of the lure, length of the line, and speed of the boat determine the depth for the lure.

Trophy fish: Fish species vary in length and weight. A trophy fish is one that is near the maximum size and length for that species. Most anglers today practice CPR (Catch, Photograph, Release) and then give the measurements to companies that create a "life-like" version of their catch to display rather than killing the trophy.

Weedless lure: A lure designed to avoid catching weeds. These lures have to be fished in a special way to really be "weedless."

About The Author

Dewey E. Johnson, the "Old Angler" in *Catching Success*, has enjoyed fishing for more than forty species with his wife, two daughters, two granddaughters, and with many friends. He has fished with world-class anglers on the Professional Walleye Trail. He is well-known as the co-author with Paul Hersey and Ken Blanchard of the best-selling applied leadership book, *Management of Organizational Behavior: Leading Human Resources*, now in its eighth edition, published by Prentice Hall.

Dewey is the author of *Concepts of Air Force Leadership*, used for years in military professional development programs. He has been a presenter at over 170 domestic and international conferences, and has been a consultant for more than 100 organizations.

Dewey served with the United States Air Force as a pilot, commander, and staff officer, retiring at the rank of Colonel. He was awarded the Legion of Merit with one oak leaf cluster together with other decorations, and is a Vietnam veteran. He is currently a professor of Management at the Sid Craig School of Business, California State University, Fresno.

Order Form

If you can not purchase *Catching Success* from your favorite book store, please use one of the methods listed below for worry free ordering. You may return any order–for any reason-no questions asked:

Credit Card Orders On the Web: www.catchingsuccess.com.
Fax Orders: 1-559-436-4866. Send this form.
Telephone Orders: Call 1-800-293-5400 toll free. Have your credit card ready.
Email Orders: orders@catchingsuccess.com
Quantity Orders: Call 1-800-293-5400.
Postal Orders: Catching Success Press, 6541 N. Ricewood, Fresno, CA 93711, USA, Telephone 1-559-436-4866.

Please send _____ copies of Catching Success.

Name: _____

Address: _____

City: _____ State: _____ Zip: _____ - ____

Telephone: _____

Email address: _____

Sales tax: Please add 7.625% for books shipped to California addresses.

Postage and Shipping:
US: $4 for the first book and $2.00 for each additional book.
International: $9.00 for the first book and $5.00 for each additional book.

Payment: Check   Money Order   Credit Card (Visa/MC)

Card number _____

Name on card: _____ Exp. Date: ____ / ____

Order Form

If you can not purchase *Catching Success* from your favorite book store, please use one of the methods listed below for worry free ordering. You may return any order–for any reason-no questions asked:

Credit Card Orders On the Web: www.catchingsuccess.com.
Fax Orders: 1-559-436-4866. Send this form.
Telephone Orders: Call 1-800-293-5400 toll free. Have your credit card ready.
Email Orders: orders@catchingsuccess.com
Quantity Orders: Call 1-800-293-5400.
Postal Orders: Catching Success Press, 6541 N. Ricewood, Fresno, CA 93711, USA, Telephone 1-559-436-4866.

Please send _____ copies of Catching Success.

Name: _____

Address: _____

City: _____ State: _____ Zip: _____ - _____

Telephone: _____

Email address: _____

Sales tax: Please add 7.625% for books shipped to California addresses.

Postage and Shipping:
US: $4 for the first book and $2.00 for each additional book.
International: $9.00 for the first book and $5.00 for each additional book.

Payment: Check   Money Order   Credit Card (Visa/MC)

Card number _____

Name on card: _____ Exp. Date: ____ / ____

Order Form

If you can not purchase *Catching Success* from your favorite book store, please use one of the methods listed below for worry free ordering. You may return any order–for any reason-no questions asked:

Credit Card Orders On the Web: www.catchingsuccess.com.
Fax Orders: 1-559-436-4866. Send this form.
Telephone Orders: Call 1-800-293-5400 toll free. Have your credit card ready.
Email Orders: orders@catchingsuccess.com
Quantity Orders: Call 1-800-293-5400.
Postal Orders: Catching Success Press, 6541 N. Ricewood, Fresno, CA 93711, USA, Telephone 1-559-436-4866.

Please send _____ **copies of Catching Success.**

Name: _____

Address: _____

City: _____ **State:** _____ **Zip:** _____ - ____

Telephone: _____

Email address: _____

Sales tax: Please add 7.625% for books shipped to California addresses.

Postage and Shipping:
US: $4 for the first book and $2.00 for each additional book.
International: $9.00 for the first book and $5.00 for each additional book.

Payment: Check   Money Order   Credit Card (Visa/MC)

Card number _____

Name on card: _____ Exp. Date: ____ / ____